D0545720

When the Belly Button Pops, the Baby's Done

"Laugh-out-loud funny.... *When the Belly Button Pops* is just what the doctor ordered for future moms."
—*Christian Retailing*

"This is the book to give today's mom-to-be.... I'll be buying a copy for every pregnant woman I know!"
—LISA TAWN BERGREN, best-selling author
of *God Gave Us You*

"Written by a mom who struggled to get pregnant, this humorous, fast-paced book is a must for prospective moms. Each of the nine months is given a chapter to cover what women will face during that time.... *When the Belly Button Pops, the Baby's Done* provides encouragement, hope, humor-based wisdom, and help at a time when women most need it."
—*CBA Marketplace*

O for a Thousand Nights to Sleep

"Funny, practical, and biblically based without being heavy-handed, this will make an appealing gift for a new mom's first Mother's Day."
—*Publisher's Weekly*

"Lorilee Craker offers wisdom, humor, and advice from the experts in her book *O for a Thousand Nights to Sleep*. She highlights the hallmark of each month of baby's first year and gives moms the lowdown on topics such as breastfeeding, baby blues, grandparents, and relationships.... Mothers will find this book filled with chuckles and encouragement."

—*Christian Home and School*

"O for a thousand more books like this one! Lorilee Craker brings hope home for new moms with this winner. You'll find honest and humorous help in every page!"

—ELISA MORGAN, president and CEO, MOPS International

"Lorilee brings humor, grace, and godly wisdom to those early days of parenting. From the fun stuff—the sweet cuddles and coos—to the hard stuff—postpartum depression and sleep deprivation—Lorilee offers the kind of no-nonsense, guilt-free insights new moms crave. Whether you're expecting your first child or your fifth, her great advice and hilarious outlook will have you feeling ready for the challenges of life with a newborn."

—CARLA BARNHILL, editor of *Christian Parenting Today* and mother of two

"Lorilee Craker is the fresh new voice for mothers everywhere! Her exacting wit, engaging prose, encouraging words, and sanity-saving tips are as precious and life-altering as a newborn baby. I have two hopes: First, that every new mother hold her baby in one arm and this book in the other, and second, that Lorilee keeps writing more books. She is an excellent writer with a warm, funny, conversational style. I highly recommend *O For a Thousand Nights to Sleep* and Lorilee's sage advice!"

—DEBRA WATERHOUSE, MPH, RD, author of *Outsmarting the Female Fat Cell—After Pregnancy*

"Almost as much as they need a good night's sleep, new moms need a good laugh. In *O for a Thousand Nights to Sleep,* Craker combines solid advice with laugh-out-loud descriptions of typical first-year dilemmas.

The voices of other moms, woven into each chapter, reassure us that there are many ways to do this mommy thing well. And above all, Craker encourages readers to depend on faith in God to get through the toughest moments with joy to spare."

—DEBRA RIENSTRA, author of *Great with Child*

"I love this book! What a great insight into all the things that come with having a baby: frustration, wonder, and humor. I especially love the perspective on friends and family and all the unwanted advice. This book is hilarious, truthful, and informative."

—CINDY MORGAN, singer and songwriter

"Every mother will identify with Lorilee Craker's humorous, honest, and down-to-earth look at what it takes to survive baby's first year. From the agony of colic to the ecstasy of that first step, *O for a Thousand Nights to Sleep* maps the course through the terrain of new parenthood. Lorilee's prose is filled with wonder, discovery, and the joy that abounds as we are given the gift to see the miracle of life anew in our baby's eyes. I highly recommend it!"

—TRACI DEPREE, author of *A Can of Peas* and mother of four

See How They Run

See How They Run

An Energizing Guide to
Keeping Up with Your Turbo-Toddler

■ ■ ■

LORILEE CRAKER

WATERBROOK
PRESS

SEE HOW THEY RUN
PUBLISHED BY WATERBROOK PRESS
2375 Telstar Drive, Suite 160
Colorado Springs, Colorado 80920
A division of Random House, Inc.

The author of this book is not a physician, and the ideas, procedures, and suggestions in this book are not intended as a substitute for the medical advice of a trained health professional. All matters regarding your health require medical supervision. Consult your physician before adopting the suggestions in this book, as well as about any condition that may require diagnosis or medical attention. The author and publisher disclaim any liability arising directly or indirectly from the use of the book.

All Scripture quotations, unless otherwise indicated, are taken from the *Holy Bible, New International Version®*. NIV®. Copyright © 1973, 1978, 1984 by International Bible Society. Used by permission of Zondervan Publishing House. All rights reserved.

ISBN 1-57856-488-3

Published in association with the literary agency of Alive Communications, Inc., 7680 Goddard Street, Suite 200, Colorado Springs, CO 80920.

Library of Congress Cataloging-in-Publication Data
Craker, Lorilee.
    See how they run : an energizing guide to keeping up with your turbo-toddler / Lorilee Craker.— 1st ed.
        p. cm.
    ISBN 1-57856-488-3
    1. Toddlers—Development. 2. Toddlers—Psychology. 3. Toddlers—Care. I. Title.
    HQ774.5.C73 2004
    649'.122—dc22

                                                                    2003022810

Printed in the United States of America
2004—First Edition

10 9 8 7 6 5 4 3 2 1

For Ezra Finney Brandt Craker.

They told us you were a girl, but Ezzer Pezzer Pops,
I'd never want anyone but you.
Thanks for keeping Mommy on her toes
and for living out such a vivid toddlerhood right before my eyes.
You are my heart.

Contents

New Abilities with Hands and Feet • Baby's First Attempts at Speech • Why Bare Feet Make for Better Walkers • Emerging (Undesirable) Behaviors • Separating Yourself from a Clinger • Faith Building at Nap Time • Finding a Caring Caregiver • Play as Toddler Work • Play Tips for Parents • Toy Story: Push Down, Pop Up!

Language Development Anxiety • Helping Your Screamer Stop • A Simple Strategy for Light Sleepers • Diving into Toddlerhood via Adoption • Opinions on Child Spacing • How to Space Your Children for Optimum Wellness and Sanity • Toy Story: Water Works

What "No!" Really Means • Life with Ez: Toddler Frustrations • The Eighteen-Month Checkup • Toddler Tutorial 1: Beyond "No!" • Effective Responses to Belligerent Behavior • A Faith-Building Prayer • Toy Story: Dexterity on the Rise

Acknowledgments

To the people who know I write in my laundry room, in my pajamas, with the dryer going for white noise, and think I'm cool anyway, my abiding thanks:

The Fam: Abe and Linda Reimer, Ken and Linda Craker, Dan and Tina Reimer, Mike and Jodi Connell, and Tracy and Lorraine Bush. George and Pat Vanderlaan, you are our Grand Rapids Mom and Dad and the finest surrogate grandparents on the planet.

The Niece: Zoe Reimer, for the wonderful toddler stories you gave Aunt Lori for moms of mellow, sweet little people like you.

The Moms: Margaret Epperson, Dawn Neiwenhuise, Alanna Friesen, Laura Finlayson, Jessica Westra, Traci DePree, Deone Quist, Ann Baker, and other hip and happy mothers who shared their stories and tips.

The Pals: Bonnie Anderson, Carla Klassen, Nancy Rubin, Stephanie Nelson, Lisa Freire, Becky Wertz Walker, Rachel Vanderlaan, Mary Jo Haab, Shari Rodriguez, and Juliana Clink for hand-holding, chick flicks, and lots of laughs.

The Newspeople: John Gonzalez, for giving me a chance, and Betsy Musolf, at the Grand Rapids Press, for your support and flexibility.

The Writers: Ann Byle, Debra Rienstra, Shari MacDonald, Lisa Bergren, and the members of the wild and crazy guild—you know who you are—for understanding it all.

The Bookies: Twila Bennett, Dwight Baker, et al., for cheering me on and giving me timely bits of advice.

The WaterBrookies: Don Pape, Laura Barker, Laura Wright, Ginia Hairston, and everyone over there in pure-air country who has been a booster of me and my books.

The Canucks: Pat Chown and Bob Wood, for everything, and especially for connecting me with the best folks on Planet Earth: Canadian CBA booksellers! (And to Jonathan Johnson, who tirelessly plugs away at his job while his bosses sit shamelessly in their office drinking Tim Horton's coffee.)

The Agent: Chip MacGregor! What a cool dude you are. I have no idea how I spent my time before I started e-mailing you! Thanks for your encouragement and for believing in my writing.

The Editor: Could I do this without Erin Healy? I think not. I am so fortunate to have you in my corner—and in my books.

The Boys: Doyle, Jonah, and Ezra—my heart and soul. I love you kooky guys so much!

And finally, to my God, who redeems me and lifts me up, time after time. You put the vision for these books in my heart three years ago. Thank You for it all.

Introduction

I must confess: Toddlerhood scares me. I've been through it all the way once with my firstborn, Jonah, and I have three months to go before Term Two ends and "Ez the Pez" becomes a big huge three-year-old. (Term Three is just a twinkle in our eyes right now as we fill out the paperwork to adopt a baby girl from South Korea!)

Right there in those parentheses, you can see that toddlerhood must not be that bad if I'm actually going to exert all kinds of effort and money to go through it a third time. Toddlerhood is kind of like labor for us moms. We forget the tantrums, the whining, and the headstrong natures of our darlings during these two wild-and-woolly years. All that slips our minds—the way our munchkins had conniptions in front of Mother-in-Law, flung their food in fits of rage, and scribbled on our heirlooms with purple marker. (Well, that one's hard to forget.)

But as time passes the whole era takes on a rosy glow, and we are more likely to remember our toddler's sweetness, how funny he was when he first started talking, and the glorious bonding time of potty training. (Okay, that was my cold medicine talking. We can agree that there's not much that's glorious about potty training, except having completed it.)

Toddlers are a mixed bag, no doubt about it. They will stretch you to your snapping point, where you will discover that you have more elastic than you thought. My two toddlers have been decidedly of the turbo variety. Jonah and Ezra put the *ram* in *rambunctious,* the *boy* in *boisterous.* Some days with them I thought I would go bonkers, and other days I thought I wanted to keep them this age forever. Actually, these emotions could fluctuate within an afternoon, an hour, a minute! You may already know how it goes.

Somehow my Jonah, who tested me with every fiber of his being, grew into a pretty cool and together kindergartner. Had I known that child number two would be even more of a little donkey, I would have run down the street screaming, my hospital gown flapping in the winter wind. But actually, Term Two was a far sight easier, even though my second son has sometimes been such a stinker. My father-in-law put it perfectly: "If God had given you a compliant, obedient child, you wouldn't have stories for your book." Amen to that! Not to mention that I have researched toddlers, read volumes about them, and had moms from Florida to Manitoba tell me how they raised theirs. All this input gave me oodles of methods and strategies to test out on my guinea pig, Ezra. Tip by tip, insight by insight, I found Term Two to be a smoother passage altogether, and now I'm holding on to it for dear life! ("He's not 'almost three,'" I snapped at my poor husband, Doyle, when he cavalierly referred to his child as such. "He's thirty-three months and still a toddler!")

I wish I had known with Jonah what I know now: Toddlerhood shall pass—and then you'll miss it! Was it Dickens who said, "It was the best of times and the worst of times"? That about sums up the two toddler years. Yes, it's scary sometimes, but it can also be incredibly fun and rewarding.

When the Belly Button Pops, the Baby's Done, the first book in this series, chronicled my pregnancy with a very lively, kicking unborn child. Then *O for a Thousand Nights to Sleep* revealed my ruminations as "stupor mom," whose bald, beautiful baby wouldn't sleep through the night until he was nine months old. But this book is truly Ezra's magnum opus, two-hundred-some pages of suggestions, ideas, and handholding wrested from my day-to-day life with him.

See How They Run is for those moments when you need some sisterly wisdom, a little "been there, done that" commiserating. As you deal with challenges from tantrums to whining, from birthdays to Barney, I hope you find in these pages some real-world traction for those days when things seem to be sliding out of control! So when you've dragged the kid out of the cat dish, hung up with Poison Control, and explained for the thirty-fourth time that Grumpy from the Seven Dwarfs may or may not have eyebrows, it's time to kick back and giggle a little at this crazy, blessed, unforgettable stage of life.

Clamor, Cling-Ons, and Clowning Around

Okay, you've just tossed the last of the paper plates from Baby's first birthday party. You're elbow-deep in soapy water as you dunk a few stray forks, and you're musing about how the time has flown since you gave birth to your angel. Wait a sec—where is the angel right now? Wasn't she here just two seconds ago? Since she started lurch-walking last week, she's been more and more mobile. A little scary! You used to be able to plop her down somewhere safe and run downstairs to throw the wet laundry into the dryer. Now you can't leave her for a second.

What else is happening in Baby's life? Dramatic hand motions coupled with incoherent babbling? Sparks of rebellion? Sudden hot and cold behavior—she wants to hang on to your leg one second and play by herself the next? Uh huh. Sounds like you've got a toddler in the house. In this chapter, you'll get the chance to brace yourself for the brave new world of toddlerhood as I introduce you to the first symptoms of the post-baby syndrome. Strap on your seatbelt! It's going to be a bumpy, but fun ride.

Milemarker: Life in the Fast Lane

Welcome to toddlerhood, Ma! Your baby (and she still is your baby, make no mistake) is beginning to interact with her world in new and thrilling, chilling ways. Her motor skills are developing like crazy, and those brain cells are multiplying faster than fruit flies in July. Those newly mobile legs of hers will take her from the toy box to the toilet and back again, and she will leave no plate unturned in her quest to explore her universe. Review babyproofing in light of her new action-oriented self and create a safe place in your home and yard where she can have the chance to live a danger-free life in the fast lane. (See Month Ten of my book *O For a Thousand Nights to Sleep* for basic babyproofing tips.)

The World Is My Laboratory

At this tender age, your baby starts to gain an amazing new level of mastery over her hands. What this means, in short, is that life as you knew it has come to a screeching halt. You thought crawling was bad? It's *nada* compared to the double whammy of walking and ambidexterity. As your munchkin's hands get busy, your hands will be even busier.

She'll poke and prod everything that interests her, which probably means anything within reach. Your walls will be decorated with Crayola scribbles and your floor smeared with clumps of applesauce (the result of the seven-hundredth version of "Hey, what happens when I…fling my spoonful of grub?") Ketchup, salad dressing, and jam are all the perfect consistency for finger painting the highchair tray—if you're lucky enough to have her stop there. Though you may be all too familiar with the outcome—more cleanup for you—consider this: Your baby learns something about the consequences of her actions from *every* one of her oh-so-messy experiments. For example: "When I send my ketchup-covered utensil soaring through the air, it soon hits the wall/floor/chair, making a delightful clinking noise. But it's only fun for about a nano-second because then Mommy or Daddy gives me the hairy eyeball, and usually I don't get my spoon back either. But the dog loves me when I do this, so it's not all bad."

Who Are You—and What Have You Done with My Baby?

Just when you think you have your toddler all figured out, he can turn the tables on you. Even the most mild-mannered thirteen-month-olds will experiment with—how shall I say it?—undesirable behavior. If your normally easygoing tot suddenly starts screaming, yelling, biting, and hitting, you can find some solace in knowing that his development is right on track. (Granted, that doesn't make it much easier to deal with.) Unfortunately, traditional discipline tactics—time-outs, lectures, swats—don't work very well for this age group, so patience and consistent repetition are the order of the day for Mom and Dad. Between keeping your toddler out of the cat food and coping with tantrums, try to take regular "parent breaks."

"I Know What You're Saying, Ma, But..."

At about twelve months, your little one will make the leap to "receptive speech," which means he gets the gist of what you're saying but can't say anything proper in return. Hand motions are the mode of communication du jour, which is why so-called "baby sign language" is so popular at this age. Unless your toddler is highly verbal, you'll probably be able to make out only a very few words at this age. "Doggie," "kitty," "mama," "baby," and "uh-oh" are just a few typical first words. Even so, toddlers now begin connecting names—"Bama!"—to the right person (in this case Grandma, who is beaming with happiness). At any rate, he'll probably have in his communication repertoire lots of nonverbal bells and whistles, like facial gestures, to accompany his babblings. Since your baby is zealous to speak his mind, he will clamor for your attention in these preverbal days by pointing and vocalizing.

Building in some free time for yourself each week is the best way to refuel your patience tank. (See also "How to Really Enjoy Your Toddler" in chapter 12 for more tips on how to avoid toddler-care burnout.)

Could You Unclamp Yourself from My Leg for Two Seconds, Please?

Having a twenty-pound weight attached to your ankle can make the most nurturing mom want to run down the street screaming—if only she could. Gluing himself to your body periodically is your little cling-on's way of making sure you are still the center of his universe. But for you, such clinginess can feel like an invasion of personal space, especially when you need to get something important done, like maybe go to the bathroom. We mothers of turbo-toddlers love our babies dearly, but that doesn't mean we don't wish they could sit and play for a while—say fifteen minutes—while we do our nails or even the dishes.

My friend Suzanna went through the cling thing with her little guy Lou. "Louis, at thirteen months, started to exhibit 'Mommy's boy syndrome' and still has it today at fifteen and a half months," she says. "If he is even just a wee bit tired or teething or not feeling well, he cries whenever I walk into the room and wants me to sit and hold him. If I don't, he crawls around my legs (he isn't walking just yet), pulls himself up, whines, and actually bawls if I don't hold him." Jessica also encountered this with her son Jacob: "He started this clinging-to-my-knees thing, an I-want-to-be-held-but-not-for-long-'cause-I'm-too-busy-getting-around cling."

But the blue-ribbon Stuck-on-You Award goes to Bethany's daughter Arielle: "No matter what I do, I cannot get her to separate from me at all. If I place her on the floor with her toys, she crawls back to me, whining to be picked up. This clingy thing is really starting to make me nuts. I love Ari to bits, but I really want to figure out a way to make her more independent." Bethany worries that Arielle's clinginess is a sign that the child is emotionally insecure and that she, as the parent, is somehow failing her daughter by not providing enough time and attention. Otherwise, she wonders, why would this little girl cling so much?

In fact, Bethany's worry couldn't be further from the truth. You could spend every waking hour lavishing love and attention on your toddler, and she'd probably still cling. Arielle, Jacob, and Lou are simply at that stage of development where they prefer being close to their nearest and dearest (that is, you and Daddy, but mostly you), but at the same time can't resist the wonders of their emerging abilities. Toddlerhood is full of push-pull indecision: "Now I want you to leave me so I can play by myself or with my buddy. Now I want to grab you around the legs and never let go."

When Arielle and Lou start to walk, they'll become incrementally keener on exploring. Jacob, an earlier walker, is already showing signs of wanting to be on his own, though he still needs plenty of clamp-on time.

For the most part, you'll just have to grin and bear it. Experts say having a secure attachment to you now will enable your baby to be more independent later. In other words, this too shall pass. Here are a few tips for those times when you can't take another moment of togetherness:

Learning to Walk

Like many musty parenting theories, the maxim about babies needing sturdy-soled shoes for walking has been thrown out the window (no matter what your mother-in-law says). Now pediatricians are saying bare is best. I know, toddler shoes are too cute, and there's no law against encasing their darling little footsies in adorable footwear once in a while. But when you're home, kicking back, let Baby roam his universe with his ten little piggies footloose and fancy free. Going bare builds necessary muscles in his feet. Plus, his sensitive soles can tell him a lot about the surface on which he is walking.

- *Ease into separation.* "I try to hold Louis for a few minutes and give him that mommy-time he craves," says Suzanna. "Then I attempt to set him down on the floor and sit next to him while we play with toys, and finally I try to extract myself from his side while he plays. It works pretty well unless he is really out of sorts. Then I just put him to bed."
- *Don't push it.* Cling-ons have to branch out at their own pace, and if you try and push your Velcro child, he may become even more clingy.
- *Take minibreaks.* Your goal should be just to get the tyke to play by herself for a little while. Like Suzanna, plop down and play beside her briefly. Once she's engrossed, get up and do something else, but stay where she can see you. Come back after a few minutes, preferably before she misses you. Eventually she'll be confident enough to let you go into another room for longer and longer periods.
- *Say good-bye.* He's wise to your ways, Mom. If you sneak out of the room the second he's remotely preoccupied, you're toast the next time you try to leave him for even a second. Instead of the stealth departure, tell him you're leaving and you'll be back soon. When you return, remind him that you've kept your promise: "See, Mommy's back again!"
- *Pass him off.* If all else fails and you find yourself willing to give up your right kidney for free range of motion, you need a break. "If Brent is home, my solution is to flee to the mall," admits Suzanna. Get your husband to take charge of the cling-on or drop the child off at Grandma's for an hour or two. Soon enough you'll be refreshed and ready to feel that precious little vice grip all over again.

Desperately Seeking a Caring Caregiver

Depending on which country you live in, daycare may be a very hot issue for you right about now. In Canada, where I'm from, moms are allowed a full year of semipaid maternity leave before having to return to work. If you live in the United States, you may have faced this issue months ago. Canuck or Yank, if you plan to work even part time, you could probably use some guidelines for finding a great childcare provider—or a new one if your current situation isn't working out.

The best referrals come from people you know and trust. Does your sister know of a wonderful at-home baby-sitter or nanny? Has your girl-friend raved about her daycare center? If you get a glowing recommendation, chances are you'll be happy too. I've had four caregivers over the years and found all of them through my church. There, you can usually find dependable, conscientious, and nurturing young moms who would like to earn some extra income by baby-sitting.

Of course you want a caregiver who has a good reputation; firm, commonsense ground rules; clean, safe surroundings; an open-door policy that permits you to drop in at any time while your children are there; and a friendly, open attitude. You want someone who will not only pride herself in taking excellent care of your child but who is also flexible, understanding, and willing to work with you. For instance, my current caregiver, Linda, has a pool in her backyard, which made me very uncomfortable. We agreed that not only would she watch closely at all times when my

Faith Builder

Get one of those cloth Bible-story books for babies. Not only do the writers tailor the very simple stories for your baby, but you can let your little one peruse them in her crib as she's drifting off at nap time. These soft books are great for naps because even if your li'l snoozer rolls on top of the book, she won't wake up. Also, as she's drifting off to dreamland, pop in a Christian lullaby CD or tape. Michael Card and Twila Paris have some fabulous recordings for your sleepyhead.

boys were near the pool—safety issues never go without saying!—but that they would wear lifejackets as well. Talking over this arrangement with Linda gave me much-needed peace that my boys will be safe.

At this age, your baby will receive more developmental benefit from social contact with other kiddies than from structure or a stimulating curriculum, so I wouldn't worry too much at this point about the educational aspect of childcare. After all, kids learn volumes of information about their universe by playing with each other! Also, don't assume that a mom with fewer kids of her own can provide better daycare for yours. Some women, like my previous baby-sitter Dawn, has five kids of her own and can clearly handle a few more with one hand tied behind her back. She's a marvel. But I once discussed a possible childcare arrangement with a woman who has only one child, and I eventually concluded she wouldn't be able to handle two more, even for twelve hours a week.

One more thing: Licensing does not always mean great care. We've all heard horror stories of licensed daycare providers who are terrible, careless baby-sitters. Of my four ladies, only the licensed one didn't work out. The others were all just fantastic. Trust your instincts more than a piece of paper!

To Play Is to Work

For toddlers, toys are more than just, well, toys. Playing is their job, a valuable means of figuring out the world around them. At this stage, toys facilitate learning and development in astonishing ways. It's fascinating, really, how differently toddlers play with various toys, and how, at different milestones, toys that used to function as dust collectors suddenly provide endless amusement and good times. A thirteen-month-old toddler will play differently than, say, a robust preschooler. Whatever her age, as she interacts with the stuff in her toy box, your toddler's synapses will fire away, building those brain cells. And here's a real bonus: You don't need to shell out loads of cash for expensive toys and batteries. Some of the finest

Parents' Q&A on Play

Laurie Sargent has written a wonderful book on playing with your child called *The Power of Parent-Child Play*. When you play with your little ones, says Laurie, they experience many developmental benefits. But how do you overcome the barriers that keep you from playing with your kids? In her book, Laurie addresses the common barriers parents experience, but she also offers joy-filled ways to overcome those barriers, plus creative, fun ways to play together and reap the benefit of good memories, closer relationships, and increased emotional stability for your toddler. In this interview, Laurie underscores the importance of play as it relates to you and your children.

Q: How does play with a young toddler—for example, one who has just had his first birthday—serve as a bond between him and Mommy and Daddy?
A: Young toddlers are on the move—quickly crawling, cruising, or waddling ducklike. Despite their urge to explore, they still need a lot of close, loving physical contact from Mom and Dad. Playtimes help provide this intimacy. Surprise "I'm gonna get you!" chases, for example, usually bring giggles when combined with a pounce and a kiss.

The best way to play with a young toddler is to get down on the floor with him. You can be your child's favorite amusement park. Play "airplane": Lie on your back, bend your knees, and as he stands on your feet and grabs your calves, gently lift high, swinging him up in the air. Your bent legs make a great slide, too. Play "roly-poly": Lay your toddler on your chest and roll from side to side slowly, saying "Roly, poly, roly, poly…" Then surprise her with a sudden log roll you do together—without squashing her, of course!

Story times before naps give you more opportunities to bond through touch: Hold the book together and let the back of your child's downy head rest just under your chin. Throughout the next year or two, your

(continued)

child will gradually wean himself from the security of breast or bottle, so he needs these predictable times each day to connect with you.

Q: When a parent plays with her toddler, how much should she be thinking about the developmental benefits of what she's doing versus simply enjoying the play for its own sake?

A: Once you become familiar with the skills your tot is developing, this will guide your choice of toys, books, and games. Then, as your child plays, you can simply enjoy sitting with him and cheering him on as you marvel at what he's learning on his own. Every day he builds on existing fine and gross motor skills: learning to place pegged pieces delicately into a puzzle or practicing climbing up and down off the couch. You can coach him sometimes, but being a cheering spectator is most valuable.

In a reasonably stimulating environment, a parent will see developmental benefits flow naturally from play activities. For instance, a basket of simple musical instruments set next to a stereo playing jazz or classical music usually inspires a tot to shake instruments rhythmically to the music or do a funny little dance in a circle. Stimulating books can increase your awareness of your child's exploding listening vocabulary. Point to pages and ask, "Where's the duck? the dog?" and he will quickly identify them. Set up a play kitchen and watch him stagger to you with a teacup. Loudly slurp pretend tea and tell him it is delicious!

As your tot grows from age one to two, he may speak only a few words, but the number of words he understands will astound you if you take time to jot them down. Talk and sing to your child throughout the day, without baby talk, as much as possible. Even chores become fodder for play and learning for your child as you talk through your activities. When folding laundry, ask your child, "Which socks are Daddy's? Yes, the big ones! Which ones are yours? You're right. The little ones are yours— and they're blue!" It's all play to him, but he is drinking in your words and learning big and little, color identification, and so on.

Q: Many parents don't feel very playful. They have little patience, they are easily distracted by all the "important" stuff that needs to be done, and their adult-sized imaginations are teeny compared to their children's. How can we become more playful parents?

A: Stop, drop, and hold still! Give yourself an award if the knees in your jeans are worn thin. Get at your tot's eye level and don't be afraid to be a little silly. Put a shoe on your head or some such thing. Toddlers are starting to figure out what things are "normal" (shoes go on feet, of course), and so they feel clever when they realize you are being silly. Enjoy these times as a reward for spending the rest of the day as the hunchback of Notre Dame, running after your meandering tot, and constantly babyproofing. Instead of seeing play as just one more to-do item, think of it as something both you and your child need in order to be close and to grow. And don't try to make play too complicated. You can often lie still and let your child lead your playtime.

Q: How much playtime is enough in the span of a day?

A: Much play can be woven into day-to-day activities, making life with your toddler more fun in general. Why merely change a diaper when you can sing a song at the same time or make funny faces at each other? But do take time to stop and deliberately play a few times a day. Grab a puzzle with small pegs or another "thinking" activity. These serve as a small window into your child's mind and keep you excited about all he is learning. Also, if you are feeling exasperated by the constant babyproofing and messes, you need to stop and play. Seeing your child reach developmental milestones during playtime will help you enjoy parenting more. If your child is hanging on to your leg and whining, he's likely to need a dose of playtime with you to feel securely loved before he crawls or toddles off to explore again. But even if you both feel fine, don't let too much time pass without playing. Your child is changing every day! Don't miss it.

educational toys available are probably just lying around your home. Plastic measuring spoons and cups, empty yogurt containers, and cardboard tubes from paper towels can open up new worlds for your little guy or girl.

Every chapter in this book offers an age-by-age guide to dolls, puzzles, trucks, action figures, and shape sorters, to all that stuff crammed in your toy box, and to how you can make the most of playtime at every stage of your baby's toddlerhood. Sometimes a toy suggestion is repeated from one chapter to the next simply because a toddler's motor skills may not change drastically from one two-month period to the next and because that particular toy—say, a musical instrument set—is highly recommended to boost developmental skills during a period of six months or so.

So open the toy box, wash out some "Dutch Tupperware" (that is, margarine containers), and call Grandma, that spoiler extraordinaire. It's playtime!

Toy Story: Push Down, Pop Up!

Gus is thirteen months old and completely fascinated by cause and effect: *What happens when I push this button? hit this xylophone? pull on this rope?* He is nuts about any toy that responds to his actions and makes use of newly minted motor skills. Push-down and pop-up toys are super for Gus. *Hey look, Ma! When I do this—push down—then this happens: It pops up!* For this little guy, toys that allow him to hit a ball with a hammer, as well as toys with buttons that trigger "Old McDonald Had a Farm" (or any other toddler Top Forty tune), are just the bomb. He's also crazy about:

- *Stacking rings and blocks.* Putting the yellow ring on the orange ring on the green ring and so on teaches Gus about sizes and how things fit together. Playing with stacking toys like blocks also boosts dexterity because it involves picking up and putting down. Show your little one how to stack two blocks, one on top of the other, and he will try to copy you. At first he will probably manage stacking only two blocks, but with a few rounds of practice, he will progress to stacking three or four blocks at a time, no problem! A bright, colorful set of blocks is a timeless toy for good reason. Talking about the letters or pictures on the blocks will also lay a foundation for learning the ABCs, although it's way too early to push letters. Just have fun building and crashing block skyscrapers for now.

- *Nesting cups or boxes.*
- *Shape sorters.*
- *Hammering sets* that let him hammer pegs or balls through holes.

My Thirteen-Month-Old

"Chloe (is she a toddler already?) shows love by making smacking sounds with her lips and sometimes by brushing up against my face with her smacks. I love those baby kisses! She also will put her head down on my shoulder and give pats on the back. So precious!"
                                                                    —Dawn

Fabulous Freebie: Touchy-Feely Toys. Show your baby items with different textures so he can compare their properties. Shiny paper, soft fabric, a woven blanket, a nubby teddy bear, smooth stones. (Make sure everything is too big for Baby to choke on.) Soon he will distinguish degrees of fineness, roughness, hardness, weave, nubbiness, and nap. Does the paper crinkle? Does the tin foil scrunch up?

Sputters, Screamers, and Spacing Your Spuds

Isn't it incredible how swiftly your baby is becoming a little guy or girl? Between fourteen and sixteen months, your kid's toddlerish behavior will start to really emerge. You'll notice his burgeoning speech, his new tendency to imitate a mule, and—my all-time favorite—the Screechies. Then, when you think you have more on your Mommy plate than you can possibly manage, pressure will start to build for you and the man in your life to procreate once more. What? Already? In this chapter, I'll help you get better acquainted with your Jekyll-Hyde/baby-toddler, seize upon new ideas for muting Mr. Screamy, and delve into various schools of thought about child spacing.

Milemarker: "Me Do It!"

Your little one's feeling of autonomy and competence builds right after he's mastered walking. He begins to think, "If I can do this, I can do other things, too!" And that's when the fun really starts. But despite Junior's budding independence, he is still going to be easily overwhelmed by new situations and emotions. Speaking of emotions, he's got tons of them and has absolutely no idea how to manage a single one, hence tantrums and meltdowns. (More on that later.) It's time to batten down the hatches and firmly yet gently enforce limits. Your growing baby needs clear and consistent messages about what he can and can't do. He will gain a wonderful sense of security when he understands the limits of his world.

Worried About Words

Now that your little bitty boy is past his first birthday, your neurotic… er…*devoted* attention is probably focused on his language skills. Words or the lack of them has sent many a mom into a tailspin of glory or worry— or, depending on the day, maybe both. "Language is the ship that sails between us," says writer Beth Kephart. "When our children utter words, we hail their extraordinary accomplishment. When they begin to speak in sentences, they introduce us to their minds, and we are humbled by what they have to say."[1]

First words, which typically pop up between eleven and fourteen months, are usually nouns such as "ball," "truck," "birdie," and so on. Somewhere between now and eighteen months, your chatterbox may even surprise you with a verb or two. ("Make," "go," and "do" are the usual suspects.)

Hey, Whatever Works!

"My fifteen-month-old gets annoyed when she's hungry and doesn't know the word for something. So I made cutouts of food and stuck them on our refrigerator. She points to what she wants, and then we practice saying the word."[2]

Next to walking, perhaps no milestone is as eagerly (and anxiously) anticipated than talking. We scrutinize every syllable that comes out of our toddler's mouth, hoping it was a bona fide word and not just baby babble. We worry when our next-door neighbor's kid is chattering in full sentences and our own precious child is still grunting like a miniature caveman. The good news is, speech development has a wide range of "normal." The smartest children sometimes don't start speaking until they are two or even three. Doyle has a cousin who didn't utter a word until he was three years old. Of course everyone thought he was brain damaged or something, which caused no end of angst for his poor mother. This cousin grew up to ace school and college and life itself, a fact I clung to when my son Jonah was not able to recite the words to "God Save the Queen" at thirteen months. Of course, as a first-time mother, I was a bit of a neurotic mess. My consternation was fueled by a woman who smugly told me her son had spoken his first word—"cheese"—at ten months. Meanwhile, Jonah was no closer to saying "cheese" than he was to saying "loquacious."

Why are we parents typically so worried about when our babies start to talk and which words they choose to utter? Many of us subconsciously think speech indicates IQ, even though it doesn't. There are many indicators of intelligence, and yakking is just one of them. So enjoy your tyke's one-in-a-million mix of gifts and abilities, which may or may not include early talking.

What a Scream!

Screeching and toddlers—it's a classic duo. Many one-year-olds seem to get the biggest bang out of hollering their little heads off for no apparent reason. Typically, this screeching business commences around the fifteen-month mark. Take this fifteen-month-old screecher: "Jacob has lungs that would make opera singers do a double take," says his mom, Jessica. "This kid loves to make his presence known in malls, where there is an echo. Just a loud *whelp!* We usually don't do much to stop it, since it is so random. We try to shush him, but he's not quite sure what that means yet." Though maddening, this drilling into the parental skull thing is not about being annoying. If your fifteen-month-old has started sounding like a banshee or worse, you're experiencing (no laughing, please) his intense desire to interact with you.

Kids groove on their parents' attention, and a toddler this age will do just about anything to get yours. Her squeals may land on your last possible nerve, even if you're one of the most unruffled parents around. I know I wondered for a time with my second son, Ezra, if I had given birth to some kind of half-boy, half-hyena. Sometimes it's just comforting to know that other parents on this green earth of ours are going through the same kind of chafing behavior from their offspring. Alanna endured the bellowing with her Bennett, and she shared with me this great idea:

"When Bennett was around fifteen months, he would sit in his high-chair and scream, not because he was angry, but mostly because he was happy or impatient. His scream was high-pitched and earsplitting! At my wits' end, I tried out a piece of grandfatherly advice from a man I knew, and it worked like a charm. The next time Bennett was shrieking, I supported the back of his neck with one hand and gently covered his mouth with the other. Then, quietly and firmly, I said, 'No screaming,' into his ear. It was a soft-spoken method of discipline; there was nothing forceful or negative or scar-causing about it! After about a week or two, we noticed improvement, and some of the screaming had lessened. After about a month of this routine, my toddler completely stopped screaming. Where I used to get frustrated by the noise and haul him out of the highchair for a time-out, this technique was far more effective, and I felt like I had much better control of my own emotions, therefore feeling like a better mother!"

Truly, this grandfatherly dispenser of wisdom should be commended for resolving a very difficult and trying behavioral glitch. (Where was he when I needed him? Hmmm.) Alanna hit the nail on the head when she suspected that Bennett wasn't howling because he was angry or trying to be naughty. Like Ez (and possibly your own tyke), Bennett was just yelling to hear the sound of his own voice and to communicate on some primal level with his peers. A spanking might have confused the issue completely because, after all, his screaming wasn't some kind of rebel yell. It was just a high-pitched "Howdy! How are ya!" kind of thing.

Another tactic to try: When your toddler whines or yells, kneel down to her level and tell her that you're listening. If the screeching persists, keep your cool and say something like, "I can't understand you. Please use your big-girl voice." You may have to repeat yourself over and over, day after day, but your child will eventually learn that when she uses a pleasant tone of voice, she's more likely to get the interaction she craves from you.

"So Are You Guys Trying for Number Two?"

It's right now—when their firstborn is between one and two—that many young parents begin to obsess about the size and shape of their family. In fact, your eldest child has only to plant her face in her first birthday cake, and people will take this as their cue to start querying you as to when you'll start "trying" again. (I love that euphemism, "trying." It's akin to blurting, "Hey, are you guys having a lot of sex these days for procreation purposes?")

"Sooooo, have you and the big guy decided when you're having your

Soothing a Light Sleeper

Between twelve and eighteen months, you may find your child is becoming a lighter sleeper. Why? By this age most toddlers have gone from two to one daytime nap; their little bodies are adjusting—and will be for months. The upshot is that your child may be extra tired at bedtime, even overtired. "His body will make up for it with extra cycles of deep sleep, but each one of those is followed by one of very light slumber—the reason he's stirring more often," says *Parenting* magazine. (Its experts suggest making a child feel more rested by putting him to bed thirty minutes earlier at night.) We all snooze most soundly for a two-hour period that kicks in roughly sixty minutes after we fall asleep. If you catch your child during the light-sleep phase, you're in trouble. Mask your comings and goings with white noise, such as a fan or soft music, or don't check on him![3]

next baby?" When people started to ask me that question around Jonah's first birthday, I was sincerely bewildered. "Didn't I just have a baby?" I replied.

At the outset, Doyle and I figured we'd "try" for another baby when

---

Voices: Diving in with Adoption

Writer Vicki Iovine, in her book *The Girlfriends' Guide to Toddlers*, muses that the powers that be were definitely savvy to give us our children in infant form. If God were handing out toddlers, "There might not have been quite so many takers," she says. "Not that toddlers aren't adorable and captivating; it's just hard to imagine devoting your life to a person who breaks your things, eats with her hands and hurls herself onto the floor if she doesn't get her way if you aren't already hopelessly devoted to the little tyrant."[4] My friend Laura, who adopted her son, Nathan, when he was fifteen months old, indeed was "handed" her child when he was a toddler. Despite the drawbacks described above, though, it was love at first sight for Laura and her husband. Here's her wonderful story:

"After all the reams of paperwork, the months of prayer and agony, and the thirty-some-hour travel time on four different planes, it had all come down to this moment: five families waiting in the banquet room of a hotel in Bangkok, eyes glued to the door for our first real-life glimpse of the little ones who would change our lives. Finally the Thai social workers began entering the room, leading frightened toddlers by the hand. Ours was the last one in—and the smallest. So absolutely adorable and so very scared, he shrank back into the lap of his social worker as we talked with him, trying unsuccessfully not to overwhelm him. The social worker would encourage him to touch us, but he was busy trying to pretend we weren't even there!

Jonah was about twenty-one months old, spacing our babies two and a half years—the same age gap between my younger brother and me.

When that September rolled around, though, neither of us felt particularly ready to go for it again with a new baby. But six months later we

"Two days later this little fifteen-month-old was ours to love and ours to parent. Already walking and talking—though not in our language!—he was full of opinions and energy. He was used to sleeping in a family bed (pallets on the floor), and it took eight full months before he would let us put him into his own bed without wailing as if we had abandoned him permanently. (In the first several months he slept through the night only twice.) His foster family had already started potty training him, but he promptly reverted under all the stress of the transition. At one point I realized that absolutely everything had changed in his life except the sun, moon, and stars. He went from hot Thailand, where he rarely wore shoes, to Colorado in winter, where he had to suit up like an Eskimo to go outside. Day became night and night, day. The language was different, the skin color of his family was different, the food was different. How many adults, let alone a frightened little toddler, could adapt to such change?

"Launching our parenting experience directly in toddlerhood and bypassing all the baby milestones has had its challenges. We missed the first teeth and first steps, but we got in on the early temper tantrums and plenty of sleepless nights. Still, we were utterly charmed by toddlerhood, as we have been by each new stage: the love for books and hands-on experiments; the snuggliness and the sloppy, sloppy kisses; the wonder of new words and new experiences. Each day has been an adventure for all of us and an invaluable opportunity to figure out how to be a family together."

were on the same baby-making page. So on our "second honeymoon" to Costa Rica, we "tried" and "tried," bless our little sunburned hearts. The result? Bada bing, bada boom! Both our kids would be December babies. (At the time, we were blithe and ignorant of such realities as planning two birthday parties the same month as Christmas.)

For me, having my boys three years apart was absolutely perfect. I relished having so much one-on-one time with Jonah, and I was energized and enthused about having a new baby by the time Ezra showed up. A three-year-old, I found, is much more mature and independent than a two-year-old. Jonah could fetch me a diaper and clothe himself to some extent, and he was almost potty-trained, too. (Yup, I did say "almost.")

Now that they are five and two, my boys play together pretty well. Maybe not as well as if they were a year and a half apart, but for me, the benefits of waiting outweighed the drawbacks. One bonus for me was that I could lavish lots of time on Jonah as well as devote much-needed time on my writing. Had I given birth to two tots within twenty months, as some of my friends have, that would have been impossible.

Now, some of you probably don't have the luxury of choosing your spacing. Perhaps you have some degree of infertility, or maybe you started your family later in life. Several of my friends and family members have suffered from the anguish of infertility—primary or secondary or both—and I am learning to be more sensitive when it comes to these things. That being said, though, many readers will be interested in the whole topic of spacing. You may not be able to space your kids the exact number of years and months apart you would like to, but you may be intrigued by what experts say about the ideal age range between babies.

One question I often hear in this whole spacing discussion is this: "Will my kids be friends and playmates if I have them more than two years apart?" (Why the two-year thing seems to be so set in concrete is beyond me! I just read an interview with expecting actress Laura Lee Bell of *The Young and the Restless,* who commented, "Everyone knows you should have your kids two years apart." Who's "everyone"?)

At any rate, I think the answer to the question is "maybe." But the answer is also "maybe" if you have your kids on the same blessed day two years apart, according to the plan set forth by Conventional Wisdom, NATO, God, and Laura Lee Bell. Spacing has almost nothing to do with how compatible your kids will be. Sure, they might have more in common when they're little tykes and both are into race cars and dump trucks, but the span of time between them has little to do with the bond they share. My girlfriend Nancy and her sister, Dorothy, are five years apart, and I marvel at the beautiful, close relationship they share. Same thing with Twila and Tonya. At five years apart, those girls are two peas in a pod. And we all know people who are not close to their siblings, no matter whether two years or ten stretch between them.

 ## My Fifteen-Month-Old

"Jacob has this little pouty lip he uses when we discipline him for touching the stove, playing in the dishwasher, playing in the dog's dish, and so on. He's all boy, throwing blocks and food across the room and banging stuff together for the noise. Yikes! But I love it and am looking forward to the months ahead."

—Jessica

Clearly, there's no right or wrong answer here, although experts such as T. Berry Brazelton and the Centers for Disease Control and Prevention (yeah, really) say the ideal spacing is about three years. Dr. T. Berry says spacing your children less than two years apart means your oldest doesn't get to be the baby for long enough. And medical experts warn that too-close pregnancies aren't good for the mother's health, as her body hasn't had sufficient time to recover and replenish the nutrients lost during her last pregnancy. Waiting at least eighteen months between buns in the oven is a good idea not only for your health but also for the well-being of your next baby. Low birth weight and other infant health problems are associated with back-to-back pregnancies.

Spacing also has implications for the emotional health of your family, especially you and your firstborn. "Having two children as close together as fourteen-to-eighteen months is comparable to having unequal-aged twins," says Dr. T. Berry. "Raising them successfully can be done, and it can even be fun at times, but it is hard work when they are little. Having two highly dependent individuals of different ages is demanding both physically and emotionally. The danger for the babies is that…the mother is likely to lump them together. Her tendency will be either to treat them as if they were babies the same age, or to press the slightly older toddler to grow up too quickly."[5] (Consult Dr. Berry's wonderful book *Touchpoints* for more on this topic.)

How to Space Your Children for Optimum Wellness and Sanity

1. When your beloved firstborn turns fifteen months, realize with a jolt that if you don't get busy in about two seconds, your children will not be perfectly spaced, that is, two years and five minutes apart.

2. Remember that three months prior, at Baby's birthday bash, you were vaguely aware of some snickers and innuendos about it being "time to try." Your friends and family were not merely referring to you and your husband resuming your romantic life.

3. Call your husband on his cell phone and demand that he materialize immediately.

4. Wearing nothing but cellophane, greet your husband at the door and laugh at the look on his face.

5. Outline your plan of spacing and notify him that if you don't "try" in the next twenty-three hours, the spacing advocated by

Ms. Becky-Home-Ecky, Queen of the Playgroup (a.k.a. "Queen B"), will be all off.

6. Try.

7. Mid-try, hear your fifteen-month-old crying, apparently up from his nap earlier than usual. Agree to hold that thought until nighttime.

8. Try again three days later. (That other night was ruined because your sister called crying about her latest breakup, which kinda put you out of the mood.)

9. A week later, get your period and realize there's no turning back the clock: It's too late to have perfectly spaced children!

10. Fourteen days and one ovulation predictor kit later, try again.

11. Try some more in the next forty-eight hours until you are rather sick of trying. Your husband, though, has no complaints. Oh, maybe one.

12. Over lunch one day, he announces that maybe the two of you should wait to add another little one to the fam. He and his brother were four years apart, and that was kind of cool, he says. It gave him one-on-one time with his parents, and he and his brother didn't really fight that much, not like those Irish twins— the one-year-apart McSweenys—down the block.

13. Stare at him in amazement and inquire, "Why, oh why, did you just have sex with me three times if you didn't actually want another baby right now?"

14. Have a tiff.

15. The next day, host Queen B and her little perfectly spaced royals to a playdate at your home. Think, *Hmmm, her kids are kind of bratty, even though they are twenty-four months and four days apart.* Think, *Hmmm, she's kind of full of herself, isn't she?*

16. Twelve days later, have your period and marvel that, really, you're not all that disappointed.

17. Hang out with your girlfriend who had a baby at twenty-one and just had her second at thirty-one.

18. Hang out with your cousin who had her kids (oops!) thirteen months apart.

19. Realize that, though your cousin's house is more chaotic, both moms were happy and content.

20. Baby-sit your other sister's newborn and experience two hours filled with rocking, pacifying, soothing, feeding, changing—and that was just your toddler. Turn in early that night and roll your eyes at your husband's lewd look.

21. Have a happy morning playing with your existing child. Decide to wait six months and then reevaluate.

Voices: Nows 'n' Laters

Understandably, people part ways on the question of ideal child spacing. Some think the older your other children, the better. That way they've had plenty of time with you and they can understand and even talk about the effects another child might have on the family.

Others think spacing your children close together ensures that they'll be playmates for life and that you won't be spending the rest of your life changing diapers. Listen to these real-world moms and decide for yourself:

"My two boys are three and a half years apart, and I think that spacing is wonderful. Since my older son was out of diapers by the time the younger one was born, I could fall in love with the idea of having a baby again. And they're clearly in different stages of life, so I don't see a lot of sibling rivalry. They really enjoy each other."

—Sara

22. Return your husband's lewd look that night and try again—just for fun.

Toy Story: Water Works

At fifteen months, Ella is "Dora the Explorer" all the way. Walking is a piece of cake now, and her attention span is growing all the time. For kicks, she tromps around the house pushing her baby stroller, with or without the dolly along for the ride. Blocks are still fun, fun, fun, especially that crashing noise when her tower of three blocks falls over. She is getting awfully attached to her plush monkey and wants to take it everywhere with her. Her favorite toys in the world, though, aren't in her

---

"My first two are three and a half years apart. That gave me time with the firstborn alone. I think the older the child, the better, because they're that much more independent and can mentally and emotionally handle the baby. In some ways I wish there were a bigger age gap between my second child and the new baby—they're only two years apart. I'm dreading having two in diapers at the same time. And I'm worried about the physical challenge of having two who need so much time."

—Pam

"My three oldest children are all about a year and a half apart, and though it was tough when they were all babies, in many ways it was great. They really amused each other, and they have stayed very close. I'm one of four children myself, and I really wanted to re-create that big-family feeling."

—Brenda
(continued)

toy box; they're in a rubber bucket next to the bathtub. If she could, Ella would spend hours in the tub, playing in the water with her bath toys.

- *Rubber ducky, you're the one.* Squeeze the rubber ducky and giggle as water squirts out of his bill. Fill up a toy teapot and pour out the water. Repeat seventeen times. Seem boring to you? Not to a fifteen-month-old who is jazzed by filling and pouring and squirting. Not only does water swab the day's dirt off your baby, but playing in H_2O teaches about its many interesting forms and functions. Water play introduces the idea of different weights: A cup of water feels heavier than an empty one. Your baby starts to figure out that water flows down and not up. *Hmmm, interesting!* A plastic boat floats nicely, and you two can make up all sorts of

"We were just mentally and emotionally ready for a second by the time Elle was a little over a year. Things went so well with Elle, and we discovered that we really loved being parents. My one sibling is two years older than I am, and I always thought that was a good distance. My husband's sisters are six and eight years apart, and that always seemed a bit too far apart to share life experiences. Besides, my husband and I tend to do things like this all-in-one intense sweep and then move on to the next thing. We thought that having the kids close would be fun for them, in terms of having close friendships with each other. More pragmatically, I have thought of pursuing a career track, so I did not want to linger long in stretching out the pregnancies. Don't get me wrong! I absolutely loved the infant/toddler/preschool stages. But I also realized that there is a lot I want to do, and I'm not getting any younger!"   —Deone

"Ray and I planned our older girls to be about two years apart. After that, we decided not to have a third child because I was working full

sea adventures. A washcloth, however, isn't quite the pontoon she thought it would be. When Ella pushes it under the water, it sinks. *Hmmm. Why did it do that?* Not only is bath time functional and educational, but spills don't matter (inside the tub, that is.) Cool, buoyant bath books are great for toddlers who love books. My boys especially got a splash out of floatable Jonah and Noah storybooks. After all, those dudes got soaked too!

- Also marvelous for fourteen- to sixteen-month-olds are *pushcarts with blocks, toy wheelbarrows, and toy vacuum cleaners.*

Fabulous Freebie: Merry Maids. Pull a sturdy chair or bench up to the sink for your toddler to stand on and let her "help" you with dishes. Fill the sink part way with water and throw in a few plastic bowls and cups.

time. I was able to quit when Abby was almost five. Then, in a reckless moment—though not without some idea what would happen—Jay began life.

"We were both done after the third baby, but God saw fit to give us another child. We had been doing all the appropriate birth-control things, but apparently God wanted us to have that fourth baby. Jared, our 'condom baby,' is two and a half years behind his brother Jay."

—Ann

"I read some parenting book a zillion years ago that strongly recommended three years as a good gap. It said something about the older child being less in need of parental time and approval, more able to play on his own, able to help, and a bit more self-secure. That seemed like a good theory. My sister and I were three years apart, and it worked for us. I can tell you this: I certainly wouldn't want to be battling a two-year-old with a newborn in the house. No fun."

—Cheryl

Contrary, Capricious, and Cute (Sometimes)

It's a good thing toddlers are so adorable, or they'd be in a heap more trouble than they already are. In this chapter, which, not coincidentally, correlates with The Age Where Trouble Starts Up Big Time, you'll get a Toddler Tutorial, your first of several installments, custom-crafted to help you cope with your stubborn, rebellious, stinky sweetie pie. Also, you'll get to peek into my world through "Life with Ez," a snapshot of my own dealings with my cherubic, pugnacious toddler when he was this age. Hopefully, when you've read about capricious Ezra and his exasperated mom—me— you'll feel like you're not alone in this world. Other children behave this way too! But most of all, my friend and fellow toddler manager, I hope you'll benefit from my toddler-tested advice in Tutorial 1: Beyond "No!"

Milemarker: Mary, Mary, Quite Contrary

Speaking of which, is your little angel suddenly using a particular two-letter word all the time? Sixteen- to eighteen-month-olds revel in their budding independence. "No!" doesn't mean "I hate you, I despise authority, and I'm on the fast track to juvenile detention." Actually, "No!" means "I'm my own individual girl. I have opinions, and I can think for myself." It can be very trying to hear the mini-diva testing her boundaries all day long, but try to remember that what she's really doing is figuring out who she is apart from you. Encouraging her can-do attitude by letting her expand her skills and try new things is one thing you can do to nurture this self-awareness and confidence. (Stand firm with the biggies, of course, like where her safety is compromised or when she is clearly testing a limit.) Once again, this means more mess for you, but don't give in to the temptation to do everything for her. She'll learn and grow so much more if you allow her to test new skills and learn from her mistakes.

Life with Ez: Tantrum in the Merge Lane

Once while driving in heavy traffic, I realized I was about to enter a sticky merging situation. My seventeen-month-old was strapped in his car seat, which was probably installed incorrectly (I'm right there with about every other parent on the planet). Suddenly my son received one of those space-alien radio signals children get from out of the clear blue yonder and announced, "Daddy juice! Daddy juice!" I had no idea what would bring up the issue of juice and Daddy right at that nanosecond, but I had high hopes that the issue could be resolved easily. As my body tensed up for the big merge, I said mildly, absently: "Daddy's at work, sweetie. We love Daddy, don't we?"

"Daddy juice! Daddy juice!" he persisted. Well, maybe not. The kid was obviously warming to his theme. "Yup, yup. You love Daddy, and you love juice, buddy," I said.

There was a moment of silence, for which I was mutely grateful as I sized up the road situation. The semi barreling down the highway would surely take my hoped-for spot on the road. Behind Bubba, about seventy other cars behaved as if the interstate were Daytona. Now at the end of my merge lane, I felt my heart sink. There was no possible way to get myself wedged into that mess of motorized steel.

Then it hit the kid: Something was wrong, very wrong with this picture. No, not the one involving the impossible merger, but the one flashing neon in his head. That is, he had milk in his sippy cup, not juice—and definitely not the yummy juice Daddy had given him last night when

Mommy was away. (It was actually Mountain Dew, a little "secret" between Daddy and him. But, you see, Mommy knows these things anyway.)

 ## My Eighteen-Month-Old

(To be read in a va-va-voom French accent, which is how I heard it when I interviewed the guy—Phillippe!—for a newspaper article.) "She is wonderful. But not—how you say—feminine? She acts more like a boy. Luna knows what she wants. She's not easy."

—Two-time Olympic bronze medalist figure skater
Phillippe Candeloro of France, on firstborn daughter Luna Nizza

He began to scream his head off just as cars behind me began honking their horns off. "Whaaaaaa!"

"What in the world is wrong?" I barked (much more barkily than I intended). But see, I was pretty uptight at the moment, and until I could safely maneuver the two of us into the middle lane, I was going to be feeling the squeeze. Because he sounded as if he might be in some sort of pain, I swiveled around to check out my wailing toddler. "Juice-ee! Daddy Juice-ee!" The kid had picked that very inconvenient moment to decide that Daddy should materialize and refill his cup with that cool liquid he had gotten the previous night. Furthermore, my darling was taking some umbrage at the fact that I didn't seem to be doing anything about it. My barkish rejoinder had only fueled his emotional indignation.

I could very well have snapped right then and there, though somehow I managed to keep it together. Barely.

Fleetingly, it occurred to me that a certain smug friend has commented more than once that she never yells at her kids. Never. Never ever. Well, isn't she special! Apparently she's *never* been at the end of a merge lane, spring-loaded with tension, in grave danger of being squished by a semi bearing the words "Bubba Done Love Trucks," all to the head-splitting tune of her screaming child. Finally, I merged, although that in no way altered the decibel level inside my vehicle. I could have, at that very moment, throttled the kid (and the smug friend, too).

Later that same day my toddler went postal when his father offered him more of the same mystery juice he had wanted so badly earlier. Mommy, having fled to Borders for a cuppa joe, was blissfully unaware that her seemingly insane child was now screaming blue murder for her and—naturally—for milk.

No. The answer to the juice then—and to the milk now—is no. Which brings me to the following application for my dear readers: Toddlers are perverse creatures, capricious and whimsical. They can come completely unglued by the word *no*. A toddler finds the frustration of being denied what seems to be a perfectly reasonable request as painful as running into a brick wall.

"No? I can't have Daddy and juice right at this moment? That makes me mad! I'm gonna holler like I have my leg stuck in the wood chipper!"

"No? I can't have Mommy and milk right now? You must be joking! While I scream at the top of my lungs, please no cracks about being fickle. True, I did want Daddy and juice earlier, but now I want Mommy and milk—*capisce?* Changing my mind about what I want is a toddler's prerogative!"

The toddler is like a mad scientist who has no impulse control, terrible timing, and lots of wacky ideas for experiments accompanied by the bone-deep conviction that they have to be done *now*. When this combustible combination meets with the inflammatory word *no*, tantrums ensue. And since you cannot reason with a toddler, don't try.

As much as they love that little word themselves, you'd think the critters wouldn't object so strenuously to hearing it. "Henry did not respond to the word *no*," my friend Suzanna remembers about her older son. "He touched everything, and his curiosity drove me absolutely nuts. If it had a button, he pressed it; if it could roll, he'd roll it; if it could open, he opened it. His persistence was very strong. I wish I could say that I've learned to deal with the behavior, but it continues today. He is not so curious in that toddler way anymore, but his defiance comes out in other battles now. At the time, I would give the strong verbal no and distract him, even slap his hand if I had to. Mostly, I just prayed for the phase to pass."

Suzanna's frustration is par for the course for parents who must constantly corral these little people who seem to have a built-in Teflon response to the word *no*. Because frustration will escalate for both you and your child if life is one big series of no's, it's good to branch out and find new and novel ways—which we'll get to in a moment—to impose loving limits.

Toddler Tutorial 1: Beyond "No!"

Darling Clementine spits out her veggies, colors on the china cabinet, and bites her playdate pal, Hannah, just about every time they get together. Even though Clemmie's mom, Amy, has tried to set firm limits with her munchkin, her efforts seem to have almost no effect on her seemingly rebellious daughter. "I feel like a broken record," Amy admits. "All day every day, I am saying, 'No, no, no!' but she still does the same stuff, over and over." What gives?

Clementine is hardly alone in her M.O. My Ez drove me around the bend half the time with his stubborn insistence on grabbing Christmas

The Eighteen-Month Checkup

At either the fifteen-month checkup or the eighteen-month one, your doc will administer the DPT (diphtheria, tetanus, pertussis) immunization and the OPV (oral polio vaccine). This particular round of needles and screams is about as much fun as the lovely two-month appointment, when you and your baby both wailed (well, I got choked up anyway). Grit your teeth and be tough, Mom, because your tyke needs these unpleasant shots to stay well. You can do it!

ornaments off the tree (and then going who knows where with them), turning on (and leaving on) the faucets in the bathroom sink, and yanking away his big brother's toys.

The one thing that finally did help—both to calm my rebellious rug rat and enable his frazzled mom to get a grip—was realizing that toddlers simply can't respond to a black-and-white no. It turns out that we parents need to exercise a whole lot more finesse to get them to pay heed to our directions.

"Like horses," says the Baby Whisperer, Tracy Hogg, "babies are sensate creatures, beings who can't actually talk but express themselves nevertheless." I believe this goes for toddlers, too, even if they are more verbal than they were when they were infants. The upshot? We have to go beyond the obvious (the kid is acting like a mule and refusing to listen to us) and identify the stuff that's going on beneath the surface.

When Ez grabs Big Brother Jonah's crayon (precipitating WWIII), it's because he wants to scribble with that crayon. Well, duh! But the thing is, he can't verbalize his wants, so he simply takes action in the only way he knows how. Adding insult to injury, he doesn't yet have much in the way of impulse control. If a purple crayon looks tantalizing to him, he just grabs it out of Jonah's hand without a thought as to what will happen next. Jonah will protest vehemently, She Who Wants No Fights will be called on to mediate, and in the end, the crayon will be returned to its rightful owner (not Ez).

Looking at the behavior of a little insurgent in this way doesn't mean you're going to let him run roughshod over his world, grabbing anything he wants, but understanding his mind-set and—here's what I know you're after—helps you find ways to respond effectively.

Effective Response 1: Distract and Redirect

Clementine hasn't thought through the fact that decorating Mama's antique china cabinet with orange marker will be very sad indeed for all involved, especially if her artwork is permanent. She is just bursting with zeal for exploration, and at the time, it seems like a glorious idea to make the furniture a little prettier. See, toddlers are not big on premeditation. So it behooves you and me, as parents of these wild things, to help them comprehend their limits without squashing their hunger for adventure. Your most potent tools here are distraction and redirection. I'm amazed at how well this combo usually works.

- "Jonah is playing with Bob the Tomato right now. Let's go cuddle the kitten."
- "Clemmie, furniture is not for coloring. Let's find your paper."
- "Ez, let's not waste water by turning the tap on. Instead, let's take a bubble bath."

Toddlers have zippo stored in their memory banks. After the crayon is gone, they're not going to think about the fact that their nemesis brother is using it at that very moment to color monster pictures. It's pretty much out of sight, out of mind with these little people. And once you've got them hooked on another idea, they probably won't look back.

It's frustrating—believe me, I know—when your child ignores your command. It can make you feel really ineffective. *What's wrong with me anyway? I can't even control a two-year-old!* But remember that "Do it

Faith Builder

At this sometimes-exasperating juncture, what better way to put things in their proper perspective than to thank God, out loud, for your bundle of energy. "Thank You, God, for Ella, for her sweet smile and cute toes. Thank You for putting her in my life." You can pray spontaneously during playtime or while in the car, or you can add these thoughts to blessings or bedtime prayers.

"In doing this, you are giving [your children] the basics of the Christian faith: God is real, He made them and loves them, He takes care of them, and prayer is talking to God."[1]

because I said so" doesn't work with this age group. Substituting shouting with a bit of creativity, patience, and understanding in your efforts to discipline will actually give you more control—and increased closeness with your little one—in the long run.

Effective Response 2: Be a Broken Record

Your tot is still pretty thick-skulled when it comes to remembering that, wow, he's actually not allowed to bite his baby-sitter on the leg just for kicks. You'll have to tell him, over and over, before the news sinks in. Also, no is not enough, as we already discussed. Amazing as it may seem, he truly may not have any idea what you're talking about: *Is Mommy telling me I can't eat this Play-Doh, or is she actually referring to the fact that I am kicking my brother under the table?*

Try to spell out what it is she's not supposed to be doing:

- "Don't jump on the couch, please."
- "That's ouchie. No touching the cord."
- "You may not hit Sabrina."
- Sometimes adding the converse—what she should do—is helpful. "You may not play with knives, but spoons are okay."

Yes, you'll still say it a million times, but she'll get the point sooner than if you say only no all the time.

Some parents are big fans of the time-out thing, but with toddlers, you may as well sing in Yiddish as punishment (although that could be fairly punishing). "Until they're two and a half or three, kids don't have the memory or understanding of cause and effect to make any sense of a time-out," Dr. Sal Severe warns.[2] (But when your tyke does hit two and a half, by all means try time-outs because, by golly, they work!)

Even while you explain what must not be done, it's still good to remove your little guy from the situation, if not for distraction purposes, then to keep him from hitting or grabbing toys.

One caveat: Keep your repetition simple. You may want to go into great detail about why Sam can't pull his cousin Asher's hair, how it's destructive and violent and hurts Mommy and Grandma and Jesus, not to mention Asher himself. But less is more here, and actions definitely speak louder than words. "You may not pull Asher's hair. That hurts Asher," followed by a swift removal from the scene of the crime, will work better than a song and dance about how world peace starts in the home.

Effective Response 3: Affirm the Feelings

When your daughter is having a mini-meltdown about not being able to eat gummy worms for supper, tell her you know how she feels: "You feel sad about not eating gummy worms, I know." Infuse your voice with empathy, too, if you can. This sends a message that she is being heard, if not heeded. Acknowledging her feelings, even her negative and possibly explosive ones, helps her feel understood and loved. Still, don't cave in, no way, no how. Caving delivers a totally different news flash: *Mommy lets me get away with murder when I behave obnoxiously.*

Effective Response 4: Praise Preemptively

Above all, heap scoops and scoops of positive attention on your babe when she's being angelic (or some semblance of it). Pay attention to and verbally notice her attempts at goodness. Then tell her about it:

- "I love the way you listened to Mommy just now."
- "Way to use your words! Yes, you may have some juice."
- "When you play nice with your sister, it makes Mommy happy."

Repeating those kinds of words—as opposed to the constant stream of ix-nays—sends the best message of all, that good behavior = happy mommy = happy toddler = happy times!

Toy Story: Dexterity on the Rise

At seventeen months Louis loves nothing more than to throw things. "Balls, toys, whatever—he just wants to be throwing stuff all the time," says his mom, Suzanna. At this developmental stage toddlers have learned

If Your Child...

Hits His Sister/Cousin/Playmate

You may feel like swatting him, which may or may not be the way to go. (I'm not antispanking, but many child development experts say hitting a child for hitting only confuses him.)

Try this instead: Say in a calm but firm voice, "I know you're mad at Adriana, but no hitting." Pick up your child and turn him away from the person he's swiping.

Pulls an Electrical Cord

You may feel like yelling, "Don't pull the cord!" or "No!"

Try this instead: If you have time (that is, the kid is not moments from electrocution), say, "No touching the cord. That's ouchie." Follow this directive by diverting him with a toy or a story.

Refuses to Sit in His Car Seat

You may feel like having a temper tantrum yourself, especially if you're in a rush!

Try this instead: Say, "When you sit in your seat, I will give you your [insert treasured toy here.]" Ezra was often distracted by a musical book with four sound chips that I kept in the car specifically for ride time.

Or try this: Say, "Mommy wants you to be safe, so you must sit in your seat." Then wrestle the kid as serenely as you can into his seat. ("Serene wrestling" is one of those things nobody tells you about in Mommyhood 101. It does, however, exist, and it can be effectively applied.)

Runs Toward the Road

You may feel like screaming, "No!"

Try this instead: Be preemptive, especially if your toddler has a habit of bolting into danger. Always take her hand when you're crossing the street, and say things like, "Always hold hands on the road" or "We have to be very careful around cars—they're dangerous" or "We always wait for Mommy when we're by the road." With enough drilling on your part, she'll get it into her head that roads are not for running. Even then, always err on the side of caution. Oversee her closely near the road, and don't let her get near enough to the road where she might be able to break away. Jonah was, and still is, completely paranoid about the dangers of cars and roads, and it's because I put the fear of God and motorized steel into him when he was a toddler.

Or try this: If your beloved baby is dashing headlong into the road and there's no time for you to grab her, go ahead and scream "No!" at the top of your lungs. Hopefully she'll stop to see what Mom's bellowing about.

the physical action of letting go, so they are grooving on the possibility of throwing. Sure, Lou can't hit the broad side of a barn yet—accuracy will come later—but it sure is fun trying. You can also have a blast with these toys of limitless fun for sixteen- to eighteen-month-olds:

- *Paper and crayons.* Soon, if not right now, your tot will get a big kick out of scribbling with crayons. Experts say first scribbles are a toddler's earliest expressions of creativity. Making your mark, even if it's just a green stripe on a blank page, packs quite a wallop when done for the first time. Nudge your budding Cassat by offering new and luscious colors to play with, naming each crayon as you hand it to her. Creating swirls of pink and purple and blue and silver makes a little one feel powerful: She can make pictures happen! Stick her masterpiece to the fridge for all to see and your little one's chest will puff with pride. (Now's the time to start drilling "only on paper" into your toddler's brain. She'll still probably mark up walls and furniture at some point, but eventually she'll grasp the fact that paper is the best spot for her handiwork.)
- *Duplo blocks and big, chunky Lego blocks* increase dexterity.
- *Activity centers* that facilitate pushing, pulling, turning, and twisting underscore cause and effect.
- *Simple, sturdy musical instruments*—like tambourines, drums, and maracas—encourage both fun and rhythm!

Fabulous Freebie: Good Ol' Pots and Pans. One-year-olds and pots and pans are as classic a pairing as PB&J. Why? Toddlers get a literal bang out of using their newly improved motor skills to pull apart and put back together "sets" of things. If your ears are suffering from the cacophony, offer other take-apart-and-put-back-together items from around the house. Empty yogurt containers, wipes boxes, shoe boxes, rubberized containers with lids, or just about anything that your toddler can easily disassemble and reassemble over and over is more fun than you can shake a frying pan at. Plus, taking apart objects helps kids understand that different elements make up a whole.

Goodnight Moon, Good Grooves, and Good Golly Miss Molly— What Are You Doing?!

Take a deep breath, dear reader. The ride's getting a little bumpy, isn't it? Between eighteen and twenty months, your babe's toddlerish ways are beginning to peak, which is both the good news and the bad news. The good news is that at a year and a half your toddler is ripe for being introduced to the life-enriching habit of reading. Inside this chapter you'll find tips on maximizing the benefits of books, plus a handful of warm and fuzzy recommendations from my toddler-manager friends out there. Plus, in the "Toy Story" section, find out how to jump on the bandwagon—literally—with your music-grooving tot. Now for the bad news. Number One: Eighteen to twenty months is the absolute worst time to fly with your toddler, so you have two choices: Drive wherever you go, or like me, suck it up and fly anyway. If you choose the latter, be sure and read my "How to Fly with a Toddler" checklist. Hey, it may help you laugh a little as you're packing. Number Two Piece of Bad News: In these two months, many a toddler in the annals of history has shocked and horrified his poor mother by publicly exploring his private parts. Hopefully, my two cents on the subject will prepare you at least a little for what may come.

Milemarker:
Darling Detective

Toddlers are inherently inquisitive, and they can and will and should make important discoveries by themselves. If you constantly entertain your toddler, she won't stretch in her ability to find out what happens when she yanks on the string or pushes the button. Munchkins this age don't get bored if they have a safe learning environment with plenty to see and do, and—oh joy—they don't even know how to say "I'm bored" yet. (That's another book altogether.) Even if your little one's attention span is like a vapor, in the right environment she'll move from one fascination to the next easily because the whole world is her discovery zone. Socially, she may smile at other children of all ages and like to watch what they are doing and imitate them, especially if they are older. I remember Jonah just worshiping the ground his three-year-old friend Nathan walked on. Everything that kid did was mesmerizing and exciting, and Jonah mimicked his every move.

Bound
to Love Books

Even before I had kids, I was a regular customer at Pooh's Corner, our local children's bookstore. One of the chief pleasures of my life as an aunt was to browse at Pooh's to find just the perfect birthday book for Michael, Jake, or Ryan. So when I discovered I was pregnant with Jonah, one of the first purchases I made was a book about polar bears for my unborn baby. By the time Jonah arrived on this planet, he already had a bookshelf with lovingly displayed, carefully chosen books.

Books provide for a quieter time, allowing wild toddlers to begin savoring the pleasure of stories and imagination. Picture-book fiction such as *Goodnight Moon* explores ideas that help your little scamp learn about the logical order of things and how characters react to events. I loved the way my boys would blurt out the endings of their favorite storybooks. It was as if knowing the outcome provided security and a feeling of kinship with their beloved characters.

Hey, Whatever Works

To teach my nineteen-month-old to use a napkin, I bought some with cartoon characters on them. Every time she's about to wipe her mouth on her sleeve, I tell her to kiss Big Bird or Elmo. Now her manners are almost perfect.[1]

"Our kids caught on quickly to *The Very Quiet Cricket* by Eric Carle," says Alanna, mother of two. "They liked to finish the sentence that is repeated over and over again at the end of every page: 'The little cricket wanted to answer, so he rubbed his wings together, but nothing happened, not a sound.' 'Not a sound' was what they would always say when it came time. Bennett, now twenty-three months, has just started doing that, and it's so adorable and fun." Obviously, a love for books is the first step toward learning to read—which happens within the shared or solitary enjoyment of looking at words.

But a word of caution: The time you spend together reading books with your little one is not really about learning to read. (If it is, in the words of Yosemite Sam, "Back off!") Toddlers are ripe to enjoy the beauty and magic of books. No longer babies, they are ready to be entertained and enlightened. And nothing beats the joy of returning to old favorites again and again, which creates a haven of love and security.

While the joy of story time is paramount, and while learning to read is obviously one desirable by-product, toddlers are developing other skills as well. For one, they're figuring out how to focus and listen—both key abilities for the future. Of course, they are not exactly known for their ability to sit still. At the slightest whim, they'll jump up from your lap and decide to zoom their trucks around the room instead of listening to how Hiccup the Seasick Viking sailed the stormy seas. You've been making the funny swishy noises he loves and affecting a most hilarious Viking accent to boot, but still your little squirtie is off the lap and onto something else. How does one impart a love for reading to a wiggly twenty-month-old? Here are a few pointers:

Voices: "My Toddler's Favorite Books"

"Jared loves all the Thomas the Tank Engine books (the shorter ones), Bob the Builder, anything lift-the-flap, and books that let him touch different textures. He also likes *What Shape?* and color-concept books. He is just getting into stories. He loves the Carl books by Alexandra Day, anything by Eric Carle, especially *The Very Hungry Caterpillar,* and anything about cowboys and dinosaurs if there aren't too many words."

—Ann, mother of Bree, 11, Abby, 9, Jay, 5, and Jared, 2

"When I read *You Are Special* by Max Lucado, my son Max says, 'Mommy, try not to cry when you read this book to me.' I get so emotional and sappy about the part where he talks about the first time he laid eyes on his child. My son asked my husband, Rick, why I cried, and he lovingly, teasingly said, 'It's a lady's job. That's what makes women so special.' I like to get my hands on any book written by Max Lucado, as he was the inspiration for us naming Maxwell."

—Alanna, mother of Max, 5, and Bennett, 2

"Both Nathanael and Adrielle love *A Mother for Choco* by Keiko Kasza, which is about a little bird looking for a mother who looks

- *Show your toddler how to look at and take care of books.* Except for my docile niece Zoe, I have yet to meet a toddler who has respect for glossy flap jackets and premium binding. Grab-n-flip is all the rage, so choose sturdy, easy-to-wipe board books at first. Their pages are easier for little fingers to turn. Keep your child's books on a shelf (bolted to the wall, preferably) where she can grab a favorite anytime and plop down for a look-see. Remove and store the beautiful book jackets. Hopefully at some point, book and dust jacket can be reunited, looking quite new and spiffy.

---

just like him. He ends up adopted by a mom who doesn't look like him, but he learns that it's the love and not the looks that matter. My kids are both adopted from Korea, so this book really hits a nerve for all of us. Honestly, I still cry sometimes when I read it. My kids look at me like I'm crazy, but that's okay."

—Cheryl, mother of Nathanael, 5, and Adrielle, 2

"My daughter Josephine loves *Each Peach Pear Plum,* which is a gloriously illustrated, rhyming story that touches on all the great nursery rhymes, like Tom Thumb and Mother Hubbard. We can be in the car, and I'll say, 'Each peach pear plum,' and she'll clap her hands and get so excited."

—Mary Jo, mother of Josephine, 17 months

"Amber had several favorites at this age. For winding down at bedtime, we often picked Mem Fox's *Time for Bed,* Jane Yolen's *How Do Dinosaurs Say Good Night?* (a fun story for acting out with hand and body movements!), and Nancy Carlstrom's *Jessie Bear, What Will You Wear?*"

—Erin, mother of Amber, 5

- *Be prepared to read the same story a gazillion times.* "I thought I was being so smart, packing a huge bag of over thirty books for our big road trip to Minnesota," my friend Ann admits. "Adam couldn't have cared less. He only wanted to read the same three books over and over. His big favorites are *The Hungry Caterpillar* and *Brown Bear, Brown Bear, What Do You See?* both by Eric Carle, and Sandra Boynton books (especially *But Not the Hippopotamus* and *Moo, Baa, La La La.*)" As Ann mooed and baa-ed and la-la-la-ed all the way to Minnesota, she soon found the animal noises and phrases engraved in her cranium forever. You will memorize excerpts of your toddler's favorite books, no question about it. I still have *Goodnight Moon* pretty much all stored up in the gray matter. Sometimes I just have to see the moon and I'll be wishing it, the stars, the air, and noises everywhere good night!

A Giant Leap for Toddlerkind

Watch out, Mom! At about one and a half, your tot will leap forward in his understanding of how the world works. It's as if someone flipped a switch in his brain because suddenly his intellectual perception has just been ratcheted up about five notches. If you give him a rather multidimensional instruction like "Go get your Clifford book from Sydney's room," and he trots off and comes back, book in hand, you'll know he's made this brain jump: He remembers where his sister's room is and how to find it, and he can keep in mind the book you requested, find it, and bring it back to you. This accomplishment may seem like a small thing, but probably even a month ago, these instructions would have been way too complicated for your growing baby to figure out. (Clearing this hurdle also means he recalls many, many other things, like where the toilet is and how much fun it is to throw Mommy's watch in it.)

- *Elaborate on the story.* Whenever you have the energy to elaborate, and as long as you have your toddler's attention, explain points of the story more fully as they come up. Also take time to discuss the pictures. (Sometimes you will be too zonked to do anything more than read the book. No theatrical, amusing accents or riffs on what's going on. Just the facts, Jack. And that's okay too, some of the time. You can't be Six-Flags-Over-Mommy every night of the week.)

- *Story time is optimum cuddle time.* Reading can be a special, sweet time of closeness between the two of you, and it is also a productive and enjoyable habit to work into your daily routine for its own sake or for a quieting-down period, perhaps before bed.

- If there's one thing I can't abide, it's the television blaring away as I attempt to read a story to my kids. Munchkins don't seem to mind a cacophony of sounds and sights in the background, but in order to get the most out of a book, *try and keep noises to a dull roar.* Turn off the television, stereo, or radio, so your little one can really focus on listening to your voice as you read the words.

- *Sit with Baby held close in your lap.* Hold the book open so he can see the pictures clearly. Begin reading.

- *Respond to your baby's reactions to the story.* Revel in his enjoyment of the tale and the little surprises on each page. My Ezra is infatuated with *I Am a Little Rabbit* by François Crozat. He loves to point out the creepy crawly things on most pages, especially the pictorial spread featuring a family of snails. "Joo-deee! Joo-deee!" he enthuses. (We have a pet snail named Judy. Long story.) Nearing the finale, Ez gets pumped up about the moon rising in the sky. I soften my voice at this point, and we talk in whispers about the moon and the bunny going to sleep. (Barron's Little Animal Series, with chunky, rectangular books about little spiders, polar bears, koalas, and so on, are durable enough for the rip-and-throw dudes at my house. Plus, the colors are gorgeous and the narratives educational. Perfect toddler reading material!)

How to Take a Toddler on an Airplane

1. Weeks before the scheduled flight, begin to fret. Hadn't you said just this summer that you would never, ever fly with a toddler again, especially not this particular toddler? Worry, pray, and mull. Wonder why driving twenty hours in a mini-van with two kids in possible blizzard conditions ever seemed like a bad idea.

2. The tickets arrive in the mail, and you realize there's no turning back. Gratefully accept a "care package" of wrapped dollar-store toys from Grandma to entertain your irascible tot en route.

3. Realize with a jolt that your five-year-old stroller, having endured seven combined years of service with two wild-and-woolly children and having been left out in the rain one too many times, is now out to pasture. Grasp the fact that being stuck in an airport on a three-hour layover past bedtime without a stroller may, in fact, be your undoing. Consider buying a new stroller even though you are done having kids.

4. On the day of your departure, allow nothing to get between your toddler and his nap time. Allot plenty of time for him to engage in the required amount of shuteye. Two hours would be premium, but you'll settle for one and a half. There, there. Your little munchkin looks so sweet and sleepy-eyed. He's good for a twofer, you judge.

5. Pack, pack, pack. Think about getting a new suitcase next time because, for some unfathomable reason, your toddler's wardrobe is taking up two-thirds of the space.

6. Twenty minutes later, pause to confirm the telltale sounds of a toddler NOT SLEEPING. Discern, in fact, that he's jumping up and down in his crib.

7. Insert wadded-up hand towel in mouth (yours) to muffle scream (also yours).

8. March upstairs to his room and tell him sternly that it's nap time and he needs to sleep now or face the music.

9. Listen to your husband casually tell you that it's no fair giving a time-out to a two-year-old for not sleeping "on demand." Wish your husband could be given a time-out for saying such a thing—and realize anew that the man has no regard whatsoever for the enormous importance of naps.

10. Through gritted teeth, tell your husband you're off to the store to buy a new stroller.

11. Argue for fifteen minutes about the need to buy said stroller.

12. Realize that, in actuality, you have no time to buy said stroller. A wary truce is called, and the baby, still bouncing like Tigger in his crib, wins. Nap time is deemed an utter failure.

Masters of Their Domains

Nothing—absolutely nothing—can make parents come unglued like the specter of their baby exploring their nether regions. Yet at this age it's incredibly common for toddler girls to rub their private parts with a baby doll and for toddler boys to check out their little winkies in the bathtubs, faces alight with goofy grins. Before you freak out completely, though, know that Year Two is a peak time for toddler interest in their little parts. Along with all the other "What happens when I…?" moments, discovering it feels good to touch certain body parts is a big "aha!" It's completely natural for your munchkin to check out all his/her bells and whistles, and it's also natural for you to feel a little, or even a lot, uncomfortable with this astonishing display of your little one's sexuality. Don't go nuts, though. Approach the situation with all the tranquility you can muster, or Mr. "Look What I Got Here, Ma!" will get the message that his winkie is a dirty thing—and that he's dirty too.

13. Pack the carry-on bag with diapers, wipes, a sippy cup, books from the baby bestseller list, snacks, and twelve dollar-store toys. Wax nostalgic about the days of yore when you got to read glossy magazines on an airplane, sip tomato juice, and chat up a fascinating seatmate.

14. Arrive an hour and forty-five minutes early for your flight and let the baby blow off some steam. Pounce on it when the gate attendant announces preboarding for passengers with small children.

15. Thirty minutes later, rue your decision to preboard and realize you have grossly underestimated the amount of steam in your squirming child.

16. Walk up and down the aisles of the plane with your toddler until the pilot announces that the Fasten Seatbelt sign has been illuminated.

17. Sustain bruises as your toddler climbs on your arms, thighs, and other body parts to clamber up and peek over the seat at whoever is behind you. Pray the person behind you is amenable to playing a few rounds of peek-a-boo.

18. Grin hugely as you realize Junior is in fact engaged in peek-a-boo with someone behind you.

19. Develop burly biceps and triceps as you attempt to restrain your child into some semblance of sitting still as the plane lands. Grit teeth as your offspring thrashes around like a crocodile being captured by Steve Irwin.

20. Respond to a poke on the head and reach up to grab a bag of candy from the stranger behind you. Throw your no-sugar policy out the window and permit your baby to inhale the candy like a child who has been starved by his own mother. (Never mind your stash of "appropriate" snacks in your tote bag.) Offer weak thanks over your shoulder.

21. Limp with relief after landing, stumble out of seat, and blockade Junior from exiting the row. Grab overhead luggage. Make eye contact with your helpful fellow passenger and restrain yourself from blithering in incoherent gratitude.

22. Chase your toddler—now tanked up on more sugar than a wedding cake—around the baggage claim area.

23. Meet your party at the gate and—whoever they are—immediately hand over your toddler. Smile weakly as they tell you how adorable he is.

24. Repeat on the flight home.

25. Buy a brand-new stroller.

26. Vow to drive to your cousin's wedding in Alaska this summer—and everywhere else you might go for the rest of your life.

Toy Story: Budding Musicians

For the eighteen- to twenty-month-old set, nothing boosts hand control and that visual/spatial thing better than the old standby, shape sorters. (You know, the classic toy where you push a shape through a matching hole.) At twenty months, Maisha's small-motor skills are being refined daily, and she can now shove the star shape through the star hole. And you should see the look of pure glee when she gets it right time after time! For starters, show your little one, as Maisha's mom did, how to put the shaped

---

Remember That Lyric

If you can't remember the words to "The Farmer in the Dell" or "Twinkle, Twinkle, Little Star," check out www.kididdles.com, which features the lyrics and tunes to hundreds of favorite children's songs.

blocks through their corresponding holes. Mismatch the shape and hole and let her laugh at the mystified look on your face. Then get happy when you manage to find the right hole. She'll copy you, and though she may run into some frustrating moments the first few rounds, when she gets it, she will *get it*.

My Eighteen-Month-Old

"Willow isn't much interested in dolls. She might pick one up, but she'd more likely pick up a telephone (real are preferred because you never know when you'll get a real person) and start jabbering away. She loves anything electronic—stereos, televisions, CD players, calculators—and she loves the animals on our farm. The first thing she says when she gets up in the morning is, 'Coat. Go see sheep, cow.' If she picks up a doll, it's only for a minute or two until she finds something more interesting."   —Traci, mother of Caitlin, Megan, Haley, and Willow

Music is a shoo-in winner for this age group too. Toddlers are all about noise. They are living large when they can produce all matter of sonic stuff—usually at great volume. Is little Wolfgang's proclivity for banging away on his toy xylophone a sign of future musical brilliance? Maybe, but who knows if the kid will grow up to be like Wolfgang Amadeus Mozart or Wolfgang Van Halen (also known as Wolfi, Eddie Van Halen and Valerie Bertinelli's kid). Even if you haven't, like the optimistic Van Halens, named your child Ludwig or Felix or Yo Yo, now is the time to let your germinating music man explore the sonic world. What happens when he clangs the blue key twice and the yellow key three times? A song of sorts—and an incredibly rewarding and exciting experience for a toddler.

Drums, tambourines, and handheld bells also make cool noises and allow your tot to investigate rhythm.

Fabulous Freebie: Aye Maracas! Got some extra pasta hanging around in a box after you've made dinner? Throw some uncooked ziti or rice into a container with a lid and secure that puppy with packing tape. (A yogurt container is just the right size for chubby little fingers to shake.) Put on a favorite CD—something bouncy and rhythmic—and maybe your toddler will even pick up the beat as he shakes his cool new maraca.

Validation, Vivienne, and Vegetables

Whoo-wee! Are we having fun yet? For me, this age span tested my limits, stretched my patience, and jumped with alarming regularity on my last nerve. No doubt about it, months twenty to twenty-two were my personal parenting Waterloo. The reason the little tyrants are so tyrannical these days? Their sense of self is building momentum, and it's outpacing their ability to express themselves. The result? Lots and lots of battles over everything under the sun, moon, and stars. The key, unpacked for you in Toddler Tutorial 2, is learning to validate your toddler's needs, wants, and personhood without swaying from your own plans. Getting a tot to cooperate with you is tough sometimes, and it can get wearisome to constantly negotiate. Here's hoping that the ideas in Tutorial 2 will give you some new tricks to get your mulish boy or girl to do what you want them to do. One big arena for battles: the table. Read about a little girl named Vivienne and how she inspired me to view picky eating in a whole new way. Plus, a harvest of notions on how to get the highchair set to nosh regularly and well.

Milemarker: On the Lookout

Toddlers are keen observers of their worlds. Experts say that babies this age spend about 20 percent of their waking hours just checking stuff out, watching people and happenings, and learning.[1] Don't worry if your budding social butterfly seems to be watching her peers more than playing with them. As she gets closer to two and then three, her way of participating in social situations will probably change. Still, it's possible that she may just be a more reserved person and not a little gadfly at all. Try to accept—and enjoy—your child for who she is.

Toddler Tutorial 2: A Little Cooperation, Please?

Toddlers definitely have their own agendas, don't they? And they absolutely operate by Murphy's Law day in and day out. Need to be somewhere—like your ob-gyn appointment—by 5:00 on the nose? At 4:45 your cutie pie will throw a tantrum over wearing his new parka. Looking forward to renting a movie and munching on some popcorn with your main man? Mr. Toddler-with-a-T will put the kibosh on that little plan by refusing to stay in his bed. Sigh. Sometimes you have to wonder.

It's as if they somehow know they've chosen the worst possible moment to display their autonomy. So there you are: late, frustrated, and wondering why you can't get this kid to comply with your plans.

There are, however, a few tried and tested methods to this madness of making even the most balking child (that would be my beloved Ez) cooperate. First, never underestimate a willful toddler's ability to shatter your resolve to remain cool, calm, and collected. True, you love the little shyster dearly, but when your ideas and his constantly clash, even the gentlest materfamilias can come unhinged. Try to have reasonable expectations and goals, such as having the diva in Angelina Ballerina pj's behave herself a good part of the time—but not all the time.

As I recommended in the first tutorial, getting inside her head for a while may help you cope with her wearisome ways. If your tot often seems egotistic and contentious, that's because she is—for now. At this age little ones are laser-focused on themselves. They're busy figuring out who they are and what power they have, and they're not thinking about other people or how to get along with them. Good news, though: With your gentle and patient guidance, she'll grow out of this and someday be more interested in cooperating.

Quotable

"When negotiations [in the baseball strike] broke down, baseball owners and players called in federal mediators to arbitrate. They should have called in the most skilled negotiator on the planet…the parent of a two-year-old. That's me. I have learned more about 'The Art of the Deal' since David was born than Donald Trump could ever hope to know."   —Jim Rosenberg

Remember, too, that your toddler is like Owen, who appears later in this chapter and whose bananas and oatmeal hit the deck in the midst of some histrionics: Your toddler's verbal skills can't keep pace with what she wants to accomplish. My Ezra couldn't figure out why Jonah got to go to preschool, play with certain toys on his verboten list, or stay up "late" with Mommy and Daddy. He couldn't grasp how certain toys worked or why he couldn't have a Popsicle for supper. Unable to express his frustration in words, a toddler will have a tizzy (remember the "Daddy juice!") instead. If we adults faced as much disappointment and confusion as a toddler does, minus any knowledge of how to cope, we'd have tizzies too.

So here's the goal: to raise a toddler who's reasonable at least some of the time.

Behold the Power of Choice

Some situations—like holding hands when crossing the street—have rules set in cement. Ezra hates holding my hand when we cross the street. He seems to be completely insulted by the fact that he has to hold on to Mommy when on or near a road. Yet time after time I insist that he hold my hand—of course. But many situations offer some wiggle room and the opportunity to give your toddler a choice about things.

At night, Warren lets his twenty-one-month-old decide if he wants to sleep in his crib or the bottom bunk of his brother's—and soon-to-be his—bunk beds. "Giving Max the option of where he wants to sleep cuts down on meltdowns over going to bed," Warren says. Ashanti, knowing that her baby Tyra is usually a good eater, lets the twenty-month-old get down from her highchair in the middle of the meal if she is fussing.

Here's a phenomenal tip that takes a little practice, but once finessed, it really works well: Create a win-win situation in which your little one can make a decision without losing face. Let's say Junior is going postal over some matter, such as not wanting to put on his raincoat before going out in a hailstorm. (You see, if it were simply drizzling, he'd be more than happy to put on his raincoat.) Instead of forcibly stuffing his limbs into the coat and carrying a thrashing bundle of hostility out to the minivan, give him a choice. Does he want to wear his new red raincoat or his big sister's pink one (since he still isn't wise to the fact that pink is lethal for boys)? Does he want to hold his umbrella or should Mommy? Often it just takes a teeny little option to give a toddler that sense of control he craves. If he feels he has some say—even if it's no big whoop for you—he's far more apt to go along with your plans.

Go Goofy

Many a power struggle can be quickly defused with some silliness and friendly teasing. When my Ez is in a huff (and he actually huffs, by the way), I say in a silly voice, "Are you a very grumpy bug? Who's the biggest grumpy bug?" He sometimes forgets what made him so huffy in the first place and goes along with kooky Mommy and her previously detestable idea about having his sandals put on. Make funny noises, imitate your child (this works especially well with melodramatic groans and complaints), turn him upside down, or tickle him. You never know if a hissy fit can be turned into a giggle fit.

Forecast Stormy Weather

Not to nurture pessimism here, but put on your thinking cap and try to envision what could go wrong. Has this situation gone wrong before? If so, it could very well go down the tubes again. Ezra used to always have a conniption when we would drop Jonah off at preschool. I'm talking dragging, kicking, screaming—it was not pretty. I tackled this problem by launching into little pep talks about an hour before school: "Ez, you and Mommy are taking Jonah and Jess [the carpool girl] to school soon. Then you and Mommy are going to go to the gym. Won't it be fun to play with the dinosaurs at the gym?" I'd repeat a couple of variations on this theme, and by the time the moment of truth arrived, Ez would be prepared to leave the way-too-much-fun preschool room.

Preparation can pave the way for smoother transitions just about every time. Try to give your child some advance warning when you're about to depart from the swing set or sandbox or wherever. Springing the bad news on a kid will only make his reaction more fierce. This technique works better the older your child gets, but start working it into your routine now and it will become second nature.

It Bears Repeating: Praise Is Preemptive

Notice your little monkey sharing his banana with others rather than swinging from the rafters. Tell him what a good job he is doing as often as you can. Validate and fortify his exemplary conduct. He longs for your attention and approval, and if he doesn't get it—watch out! He'll be naughty just to get your eyes focused on him again. Every time twenty-month-old Elliot sits calmly in his car seat instead of whining or thrashing around like a wild thing, his dad says, "Way to sit like a big boy in the car, buddy." Elliot beams, thrilled to have pleased his dad and earned his validation.

Getting your toddler on the same page as you is often a two-steps-forward, three-steps-back process. But sometimes a strategy works like a charm, and when it does, you will have gained a small step forward in your quest to get your sweetie to go along with you. One of these days (the day before he turns three, no doubt), you'll figure it out, and both of you will be closer for having explored the possibilities.

Picky Eaters Versus the Vivienne Principle

I'll never forget eating dinner with Vivienne, a young lady of two with astonishing culinary daring and sophistication. One night my family dined with hers at an authentic Indian restaurant, a place frequented by Vivi's parents, Wanda and Aaron. Jonah was about two and a half at the time, still moldable in terms of his eating habits—one would think. My toddler ate the flatbread, a few particles of rice, and one piece of curried chicken. He was too busy staring, open-mouthed, at his little pal Vivienne's plate, heaped with palak paneer—a green, liquid substance of pureed spinach and cheese—which was disappearing as fast as Vivienne could shovel it in.

Now, trying new and exotic foods is generally fun and adventurous for adults. Most of us like a little variety to wake up the ol' taste buds. (I quite enjoyed the green, liquid substance and vowed to quit being such a big, fat clucking chicken when it comes to experimenting with ethnic foods.) Toddlers, of course, have a different mind-set. The broadening of their culinary horizons is to be resisted at all costs. When it comes to eating, the toddler mantra goes like this:

> I will only eat that which is appealing to me at that nanosecond
> in time when you present it to me. Those options may or may
> not include bananas, hot dogs, mystery-meat nuggets, cereal, and
> peanut butter and jelly sandwiches, crusts off. A Happy Meal is
> okay too, if accompanied by a useless plastic toy from a movie I'm
> still too young to see. Ice cream is good for all meals as well. Other
> than that, I won't eat a thing, even if you coax, cajole, plead, and
> bribe me.

Of course there are exceptions to this rule, Vivienne being a dazzling one. "She won't eat 'American' food," Wanda sniffed. A little uppity, I thought, although who could blame her? "All she eats is Indian, Thai, and Lebanese food. Baba ghanoush is her favorite." Meanwhile Jonah continued to look at Vivienne as if she were spooning alien intestines into her mouth. I knew then that even with peer pressure on my side, Jonah wasn't going to ingest the green stuff unless force-fed with a tube. Even the curry chicken had been a stretch.

I left the restaurant discontent with the knowledge that somehow I had failed to instill in my child the same appreciation for global culinary experiences that Wanda had instilled in hers. Still, I did learn something from that luncheon, and I have come to call it the Vivienne Principle. The principle goes like this: Just as Vivi ate and grew accustomed to whatever foods she was offered, so too would any munchkin with an impressionable palate eat what was put in front of him. The key is to start early. In the womb Vivi became acclimated to Wanda's penchant for coconut milk, satay, and hummus. Après womb, Mom's breast milk was infused with curry and all kinds of global spices, and by the time little Vivienne could eat finger foods, all she knew was exotic eating. To her a PB&J tasted outlandish, while a pita stuffed with falafel was all that and a bag of chips (dried radish chips, of course).

As I see it, according to the Vivienne Principle, no food is really weird unless that's how it is presented by Mommy and Daddy: "You are really going to turn your nose up at this, buddy, because it's tuna, and tuna is known to be blacklisted by four out of five children under the age of five. But because I think you should cut down on hot dogs and because tuna is good for you, I am now going to give this to you. You're not going to like it one little bit, but here goes."

Would you eat something if the person who gave it to you was cringing and grimacing? Of course not! Yet that's often how we pitch new foods to our kids. It's either too negative a presentation or a wildly optimistic one: "You are going to *love* this broccoli casserole! It's stunning—STUNNING!

Your little taste buds are going to just *explode with joy* when you take a mouthful of this treat. And guess what? You know Big Bird? This is his *favorite* dish!"

Basically, any new foods should be unveiled with a carefully cultivated air of casualness. The right attitude is one of calm, of serenity, of obliviousness to any reason why anyone would dislike a food prepared by you. Unlike Wanda, bless her granola soul, we sometimes make assumptions about what kids like to eat because that's what kids from time immemorial have supposedly liked. But hey, actual Indian, Thai, and Lebanese children eat the foods of their cultures, obviously. It's yummy to them (and Vivienne), so why wouldn't it be yummy to our kids? Because if you open up the cultural baggage of our white-bread worldview, you'll find it filled with hot dogs, pizza, peanut butter, and Cocoa Puffs! Do kids like that stuff? Of course they do. Would they like some variety in their diet if it were presented early enough and positively enough? They just might.

Take, for example, my two sons. I assumed Jonah wouldn't like salad, so I rarely offered him anything leafy and green. Instead he would get cooked carrots or peas, and Doyle and I would eat salad. Of course I had less time to devote to short-order cooking when Ezra came on the scene. So when he was old enough to join us at the table in his highchair, I just gave him a little of whatever we were having. Lo and behold—that kid eats more salad than anyone else. And naturally he likes his greens good and doused with Ranch dressing, which he licks off the lettuce, but hey, it's salad!

Better Than Beige: Tips for Enticing Baby to Eat a More Colorful, Balanced Diet

- *Vegetable subterfuge.* Slather those veggies with melted cheese (real cheese, please) and that woeful Brussels sprout just may make it down the hatch. Writer Michelle Kennedy offers this great tip for marketing veggies: "For raw vegetables, cut them up long and thin and give your kids some dips, like mayo or cheese 'n' onion. Guaranteed a success—they simply love 'em!"[2] Make faces with vegetables, kabobs with fruit and cheese. Blather on incessantly about Bob the Tomato and Larry the Cucumber. Display vibrant enthusiasm about vegetables—think like a PR chick for the broccoligrowers association—and maybe your radish-resistant tot will start to have an open mind. Little guys also appreciate the in-control feeling of dipping their food or smearing something on it. (Also, see the "Fabulous Freebie" on plastic picnic knives in chapter 6.) Cater to their urge to be in control by offering all kinds of dips and spreadables like yogurt and cream cheese. It's amazing what kids will eat when they've doctored it up a little.

- *So smoothie.* The cool thing about blended foods is that your child will have no inkling that his delicious smoothie also has carrot juice, leftover broccoli, and whatever else you feel like throwing in there. "Everything (and I mean everything) my son doesn't eat in a day goes into a blender with fruit, juice, yogurt, or a little milk, and a dose of his vitamins," says Michelle Kennedy. "He finishes every drop before bedtime and none ever goes to waste."[3] Sound gross? Maybe so, but it really does work! Up the ante even more with fun cups and squiggly straws.

- *Put it in reverse.* Reverse psychology, used sparingly, works like a charm. Grandma Pat uses this tool effectively with my boys. "It's time for a nap now, but don't you dare fall asleep!" she likes to chirp as they are fighting a midday siesta. They always look at her, wide-eyed and puzzled, and sometimes they even take a nap just so they can prove her wrong! The same perverse principle works for eating. Toddlers are famous for being possessive of "their" stuff, which can include the very food on their plate. Try saying, "Can Mommy eat your carrots?" Mr. Pickle Face might suddenly warm up real fast to "his" veggies.

- *It's baloney!* Not to be uppity (after I just dissed on Wanda for being a tad smug about her child's eating), but I keep hot dogs and baloney to a minimum. These mystery meats are not even good for your child, besides the fact that they offer only a little low-quality protein. Furthermore, the chemicals in hot dogs have been linked to cancer in small children, and as far as meat goes, it's not even really meat, technically. One day on a whim I decided to offer Ezra a slice of baloney to see what he would do. *He probably won't even like it,* I thought smugly. *Then I can report to all my readers that small children don't actually enjoy heavily processed meat by-products. They just have a reputation for liking it.* Ezra adored the baloney. He pleaded for more and more of it until he had just about wolfed down the whole package. So my grand experiment had failed quite miserably, true, and I had to report something entirely different to you (which you already know): Small children love nothing more than to eat meat made from indeterminate pig body parts. However, that doesn't mean we should feed it to them. Vivienne notwithstanding—her taste buds are jaded by all that baba ghanoush—toddlers can be led to enjoy alternate sources of protein, such as…

- *Peanut butter wonder.* It tastes great, and kids are nutty about the stuff. Throw some sliced bananas in a sandwich and cut it into a shape with a cookie cutter—voilà! Little kids eat anything in shapes. Spread some on whole-wheat flatbread or in a pita with fruit spread. Smear a glob on some crackers for a wholesome snack or use it as apple dip. It's good food—and, hey, kids like it—but it shouldn't be your toddler's only source of protein. It's actually only 25 percent protein and 48 percent fat. It's also low in key minerals like zinc and iron found in complete animal proteins such as cheese, eggs, soy milk, and beans. Natural peanut butter—made with only peanuts and salt, and none of the sugars or hydrogenated fats—is best and can be found in most grocery

stores right alongside the other peanut butter spreads. Peanut allergies can be lethal, too, so make sure Junior's not allergic before you
start giving him PB&Js for lunch. (How do you know if your
toddler is allergic to peanuts? Some experts go as far as to say you
shouldn't expose your child to possible allergens until they are
thirty-six-months old. In my opinion this is a bit extreme, but
consult your pediatrician about his or her view. If both you and
your husband have allergies, the chance of your kids having allergies is high. Proceed with caution when introducing a highly
allergenic food like peanuts.)

- *Cheese.* Toddlers are little cheeseballs who love this wonderful,
  nutrient-rich food in almost any form. I buy three bags of shred-
  ded cheese at a time and throw it on just about every food that
  doesn't have chocolate in it. Scrambled eggs, tuna melts (which
  sneak in a good portion of brain-boosting omega-3 fatty acids and
  vitamin E), tomato soup, salad, veggies—anything that can possibly benefit from a layer of cheese gets it. Because children also
  love anything rolled—I think they might eat dried okra if it were
  rolled in something—I add cheese to tuna or turkey roll-ups and
  even just plain roll-ups. Cheese sticks are also fabulous snacks.
  Throw in a cereal bar and you've got a small lunch-on-the-go.

- *Put the squeeze on juice.* Judging by the plethora of juice commer-
  cials on the tube, you'd think it's a wonderful source of vitamins
  and little kids should be drowning in it. But juice is just riddled
  with sugar. (My friend's husband lost fifteen pounds simply by
  cutting juice out of his diet.) Too much sugary juice means your
  tot fills up too fast and won't be open to eating whole fruits, never
  mind veggies. Even 100-percent fruit juices are generally considered less nutritious than whole fruits, which contain valuable fiber
  and vitamins stripped in the juicing process. Unlike juice, an apple
  has micronutrients, fiber, potassium—lots of great things you don't
  want your child to miss. (Apple tip: One of the most cherished

items in my larder is the little contraption which—in one fell swoop—slices an apple into eight perfect wedges. No coring! No wedging! No choking on seeds! And my guys dig their apple snacks.) My Ez, as you have learned, loves and adores juice and has a coronary if he can't have any or is offered milk or water. I have been slowly weaning him of this desire by diluting the juice gradually. Now I am basically giving him flavored water. Another idea is to throw some colorful juice ice cubes into a cup of water. Toddlers are fascinated by novelty, and purple grape-juice ice cubes floating in water probably qualify. If it's not already too late, don't offer juice to your toddler. A friend of mine never even started giving her little girls juice—ever! They drink only milk and water and have none of the wrestling matches you and I have had.

- *Milk it.* Lactose intolerance is extremely rare in children under three. If as a baby your child was diagnosed with a milk allergy, as my Jonah was, give him Vitamite or some other milk-free dairy drink. Some of them are kind of nasty, but Vitamite actually tastes pretty good. Chocolate milk is great for kids who don't like the unleaded stuff, but don't overdo it or you'll be running to the store at 9:00 P.M. for chocolate milk—as if you weren't going there anyway for wipes or diapers. Yogurt is a calcium-rich snack too, and kids generally gobble it up. If your child has a small appetite but high-energy demands, give him whole milk to drink for extra calories.

- *Custom feeding is a-okay.* Remember, every toddler is different. "One thing we are finally figuring out is that Adrielle is all about FOOD," says my friend Cheryl. "When her brother, Nathanael, was two, he lived on juice and air. He never ate. Adrielle grazes all day long. A lot of times her behavior deteriorates because she's starving. We're starting to clue in that she really needs four meals a day and that one of those meals should be at 3:30 or 4:00. That way, she's not just eating crackers and raisins and chips from 3:00

(end of nap) to 6:00 (dinner) and then not eating dinner." It can be tempting to offer frequent snacks as a way to avoid a toddler meltdown or tantrum. But all kinds of snacks can overload your toddler with sugary carbohydrates and fats, plus cause him to come to dinner with little appetite, a recipe for picky eating. You know your cutie better than anyone. Maybe, like Adrielle, your toddler needs to eat more than three square meals a day. Or possibly you have a Nathanael, with the energy of a rabbit and the diet of a mouse. Customize your food strategies appropriately.

- *Variety is the spice of life.* Owen always, always ate bananas and oatmeal for breakfast. It was his parents' one surefire meal of the day. "Even if I knew Owen might fight us at lunch or dinner, he would definitely eat his favorite breakfast," says his mom, Reanne. But one day he shoved the entire meal on the floor. "No nanas, Mommy. No nanas!" he howled. Toddlers, like adults, sometimes need a change of pace even when it comes to set-in-stone food faves. There's no accounting for the eccentricities of a toddler's appetite. One day the kid wolfs down bananas as if they were candy. The next, ix-nay on the bananas unless you let him peel it himself—oh joy. The point is, he can't talk yet, at least not like you can, so it behooves you to try to read his mind a little here and there. Don't be surprised if yesterday's filet mignon is tomorrow's road kill.

Faith Builder

Disciplining our children has a spiritual dimension as well as a practical one. When our children learn to obey us, we build into their hearts that they should obey Jesus as well. Connect the two whenever you can: "Carys, when you obey Mom and do what I ask, you are making Jesus happy too!"

- *One-plate special.* Many parents make a point of offering their toddlers a variety of choices even if their children don't have the patience for it. In cases like this, the battle that ensues may have nothing to do with food itself; the toddler is just exercising his desire for control. The best way to win: Step out of the ring. Offer your demi-diner one plate with a balanced meal on it. If he turns it down, it's okay for dinner to be over. One missed meal won't kill anyone. (As for those undesirable leftovers, see "So Smoothie" above.) When your child won't try something new, don't hesitate to offer it again a few days or weeks down the road. Presentation or preparation can also make a difference. A kid may like hamburgers, but not meatloaf, for instance. When you reintroduce an item, don't make a big deal out of it. Just put it on the table and dig in.

Whaddya Mean "Sit Still"?

Sitting still while Mommy and Daddy finish their dinner doesn't sound like too much to ask, does it? Not for you, a fully socialized, grown adult. But your toddler can find it maddening to sit still while you and your husband catch up on your days. Your toddler may brandish a fork and spoon like a pro and drink out of a cup without spilling, but that doesn't mean mealtimes are smooth sailing just yet. She may be more interested in conducting little science experiments on her tray table—like pouring her grape juice into her ravioli—than eating. Or she may insist on sitting on your lap and eating what's on your plate rather than what you've placed in front of her. (See "Life with Ez: The Little Turkey" in the next chapter.)

When Jonah was this age, suppertime became a nightly power struggle between him and us. He wanted to get down five minutes after he started eating, and we wanted him to stay put for at least fifteen. What I know now is that you can't expect a twenty-three-month-old—still a baby for another month, technically—to calmly wait while you blather on about grown-up stuff. *Not only do I have to sit trapped in this highchair, but no one even remembers I'm here!* Be sure to include your little one in the conversation as much as possible. Consider feeding him while he sits in a toddler-sized chair at a small, low table, and serve a variety of finger foods that he can handle by himself with ease. If he just can't sit still for the duration of an adult meal, feed him first and then let him play while you relax and enjoy eating the rest of your meal.

Toy Story: Pretending and Painting

In his race toward independence, twenty-two-month-old Ned sometimes bites off more than he can chew. His parents, Olivia and Peter, try not to take over when Ned is struggling with a toy. They praise his attempts to put together tray puzzles or arrange plastic people in his toy bus, and they offer help only sometimes. "The more Ned can put that puzzle together by himself, the more he is just thrilled with himself and his achievement," says Peter.

The Quiggles have also noticed that the less they intervene, the more Ned's imagination will take over. When he's playing with his big red fire truck, for instance, and can't figure out how to turn on the siren, he'll soon be making his own siren noises. Experts say encouraging pretend play is a huge boost to developing the almost-two-year-old's imagination. Toddlers at this age will start to *vroom! vroom!* around the room, riding their imaginary cars or racing their toy vehicles. My niece Zoe pretends to pour tea from a toy teapot into a cup. She hands Oma the cup and expects her to take a ladylike sip. When Ned is arranging his little plastic people in the school bus (sometimes they end up upside down or sideways, but who cares?) or when Zoe serves Oma from her toy tea set, they are beginning to see the contrast between what's real and what's not. Pretend play is the beginning of the wide-eyed wonder years of childhood—a beautiful thing!

Finger paints add to the wonder. Deliciously messy and touchy-feely, finger painting is your toddler's entrée into the world of color exploration. What happens when I smush the blue and the yellow paints? Green! The orange and the green? Nondescript brownish gray! Will the big part of my hand make a different shape than my finger does? For a new shape and sensation, get your tyke to wriggle her toes in a pool of paint and then walk on paper. She'll love it! When the weather doesn't allow for backyard painting sprees, spread a splat mat or an old tablecloth or sheet on your kitchen floor for easy cleanup. Even more fabulous: bath paint. I'm a huge fan of this bath paint stuff. Ez got some for Christmas (it makes a super fun and economical gift for all the toddlers on your list), and we had a ball squishing and smushing and swirling and smearing all over the bathtub. The best part is, it washes away with the bath water.

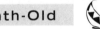

My Twenty-Two-Month-Old

"Judah eats anything with carbs in it. He would eat pancakes morning, noon, and night if we let him. When I say, 'What do you want for lunch?' he's like, 'Pancakthe! Pancakthe! Pancakthe!' He eats any and all starches, and he repeats everything he says a hundred times—even if we answer him right away. So we have two nicknames for him: Carbo and Repeato."   —Margaret

Fabulous Freebie: A Dab'll Do Ya. Cover up the bathroom floor with towels and strip your toddler down to her diaper while you run a bath. With bath paints (or really any washable, nontoxic paint), use your finger to paint a green swirl on your child's ears, red stars on her knees, and a smiley face on her adorable toddler tummy. As you decorate your child, sneak in a little body-parts lesson: "Here's your nose, and what's this? Your toes!" If your little girl is a can-do type, she might want to participate in the artistic process. Let her smear some pink on her arms or legs—or on yours! When the bath is full of bubbles and you think it's time for a scrub, just dunk your painted patootie and she'll be as clean as a whistle (however clean that is). It just may rank as the most fun bath ever.[4]

Turkeys, Tantrums, and the Big Two

Your little one is almost two! Unbelievable! But don't let that whole "Terrible Twos" business scare you. My firm opinion is that the worst of toddlerhood is just about behind you. Both my wild things seemed to calm down ever so slightly around two, and they kept getting more manageable after that.

But here you are, still buffeted by the hurricane, so to speak, and still in need of some tips to get you through the rough patches. Voilà! Toddler Tutorial 3 is here to help you cope with tantrums, that oh-so-notorious toddler activity since time immemorial. You'll learn why toddlers have tantrums, how to respond, and how to assist your out-of-control child with gaining hold of her emotions. But first—speaking of rough patches— you'll peek into my sometimes-turbulent world with another installment of Life with Ez: The Little Turkey. Finally, as you approach the big day when your baby turns two, you can smirk at me as I poke fun of myself— and of many other mothers of two-year-olds—for planning an elaborate celebration for someone who will probably cry or nap his way right through it! Go ahead and throw a party for your two-year-old anyway. You'll live to tell a hilarious tale.

Milemarker: Word Combos

Your toddler can probably hum now and sing smatterings of songs such as "Twinkle, Twinkle, Little Star" and make three-word sentences like "Kitty run out." She can likely follow a two-step request such as "Come here and turn around so I can comb your hair." Many twenty-three-month-olds love identifying opposites: tall man, short man; big hot dog, little hot dog. But if your toddler isn't doing all these things, don't worry. Children learn to speak at different rates, and your child may still be working her way up to this stage.

Life with Ez: The Little Turkey

The Craker family was anticipating a lovely Thanksgiving. I was going to plunge into my annual culinary expedition (autumn being the only time I get the yen to do more than fix something edible). I had found a doable dump-'n'-stir recipe for pumpkin soup, Doyle was looking forward to hitting the sweet potato casserole with gusto, and Jonah was running around naked, save for a "skirt" made out of a dishtowel and a homemade Indian headdress with little feathers stapled to a ring of construction paper. Ezra was just happy to be going to visit "Bama" and "Bampa."

Thanksgiving always begs the question "What are you grateful for this year?" Well, I for one was beholden for two robust little boys, boys I had missed the previous weekend when I had flown to Colorado for a pal's wedding. Yes, they were currently sporting vestiges of dried snot from lingering colds. True, every five minutes a fight would break out over a matter of utmost importance, such as the little one "crinkling" the big one's paper airplane (one of seventy-five littered around the house). Still, on balance, I had many reasons to feel fortunate.

That was at the beginning of the day.

By the time grace was spoken and family members began to sip delicately at their watery first course (What had I done wrong? The "dump" or the "stir"?), it became clear that rather than eat the turkey, my Ez would do his best imitation of one.

He didn't want to sit in his seat. He wanted to sit on my lap and be fed morsels from Mommy's plate.

Calmly I explained to him that he had to sit in his seat. Otherwise he would have to go take a nap. This went over like a deflating blimp at the Macy's parade.

A mini-tantrum erupted with tears and the word *no* vehemently repeated about seventeen times.

I eyeballed Doyle, who was already heartily digging in to his meal. He shrugged with a look that implied, *Who knows what to do at a time like this?* Besides, there was the engorging of holiday victuals to be done.

Well, someone needed to save the situation. I removed my wailing son from the epicenter of activity and tried to reason with him in a quiet, private place. "Ezra," I said sternly, "you have to sit nicely and eat, otherwise it's going to be time for a nap." (Though he had slept for about an hour on the car ride over, it was obvious this interlude hadn't staved off serious crabbiness.)

He sniffled unhappily. "No," he said softly, wiping his runny nose with his sleeve.

"Do you want a time-out?" I said, realizing this was in fact the most rhetorical question known to toddlerkind.

"No!"—this time a little louder.

"Okay then. You sit nice and eat your food."

We returned to the table a grim pair. I knew this would not be the end of it.

People began to pass me things I had missed while I was attempting to discipline my child. "Gravy?" Sure, although I had nothing to go with it yet. "Cranberry sauce?" "Turkey?" In a few moments, my plate was assembled, heaped beautifully with all manner of holiday decadence.

"I'm all done," my twenty-three-month-old announced, glaring at me.

Ignoring him, I started gobbling my food, already in the first stages of cooling. I knew full well that if I let him, the little crumb-snatcher would ruin my meal.

"Ez," Doyle piped up, "if you get down from the table now, you can't eat anything else. No pie."

I knew my son had to be hungry, and he was just pulling this mutiny to, well, to do what toddlers do: assert themselves as individuals. This was shaping up to be a classic power struggle. And it was playing out in front of the in-laws no less.

Family dynamics were ricocheting all over the dining room. I love my in-laws. All of 'em. But I had to deal with the whole "cooking for Martha Stewart" feeling whenever I made something for my domestic-goddess mother-in-law (who is always as gracious and encouraging as can be, but still…). So that little factor had already put me slightly on edge. Then there was the classic generation gap thing as far as discipline goes. How far would I let this twenty-five-pound kid push me? This query hung in the air like pollution over L.A.

"Eat your food," I tried, lamely. "It's yummy."

"All done," he said, already scrambling down from his booster seat. He ran over to me and attempted to climb into my lap.

"Ez, you can't sit in Mommy's lap right now. Mommy is trying to eat."

Eating with a wildly unpredictable toddler who has a special talent for knocking over crystal glasses was not my idea of a relaxing holiday feast. Besides, he had to learn to sit at the table just like at home.

"Lap! Lap! Lap!" Ez began to cry again.

Sigh. I felt *this close* to caving in to his demands, only so I could eat more than a few measly mouthfuls of the bounty spread before me. Weak. Very, very weak was I at that moment.

Where was the child's father during this wrestling match? Stuffing his face, of course, oddly oblivious and definitely unhelpful. Yes, I found this quite irritating. Family dynamic number forty-two: Around his family, Doyle sometimes reverts to the boy he once was instead of remaining the man I married. In his defense, he wasn't feeling well, which got him off the hook. Sort of.

"Doyle," I said through gritted teeth, "do something."

Having just read in an august childcare manual that a parent should never "allow [the toddler's] antics to disrupt the entire family," I was beginning to develop a complex.

Lousy Cook. Nagging Wife. Ineffectual Mother. Have mercy. Pass the pie.

Doyle sternly told his son to get back in his chair or risk losing his piece of the pie, so to speak. That little intervention worked about as well as my soup recipe.

I'd like to report that a brilliant solution was found *toute de suite* and that Ezra complied with our fervent wishes for a peaceful dinner.

I'd like to report that.

But somewhere between insanity and pie, I did waffle and allow my intractable tot to sit on my lap, where he proceeded to eat his Thanksgiving dinner off my plate.

More tugs-of-war followed, over how much whipped cream Ez could have on his pie, over being told not to play with Mommy's "foffee" cup because it was bone china, and over his wanting to "help" dry the dishes— more chances for shattered heirlooms! I ended up wetting a bunch of plastic cups and giving him a dishtowel, which was the best idea I had all day long.

By evening and the car ride home, I felt about as wrung out as that towel I had given Ez. *What kind of mother couldn't control her own child?* I thought miserably. And if the little tyrant had to exert his autonomy, why so strenuously—and why, oh why, today, Thanksgiving, with a bunch of relatives witnessing every skirmish?

At least he wasn't whining or squawking or screeching right at that moment. In fact, I hadn't heard a peep from him in quite a while. I swiveled in the front seat to see what on earth my vexatious son was up to.

Despite myself, the sight of Ezra fast asleep in his car seat caused me to thaw—a little. Of course he would sleep now. After all, he hadn't had his proper nap today, and now he was confined to a warm and humming car seat. A lock of his silky blond hair fell over his forehead, and his chubby cheeks were still pink from being out in the cold air. *Little Ez the Pez*, I thought, *my baby*. My resentment started to melt, and in spite of myself my heart welled up with love for my fractious, exasperating toddler. How angelic he looked snoozing contentedly, his sweet head snuggled in the soft lining of the car seat.

Yes, he had given Mom a run for her money today. He had pushed me and my limits with all the might of his flinty will, but at least I had a toddler to test me. I reflected on Doyle's sister and brother-in-law, who had desperately wanted a baby for years and years. They would probably never get the chance to go ten rounds with a pugnacious little boy of their own. I wondered if that's what they were thinking as they observed their nephew's belligerence over dinner.

I sighed. Tomorrow would be another day and another chance to get in the ring with Ezra. It would also bring more chances to hold him close, kiss his toes, and tell him I loved him more than life itself.

Yes, he behaved like a little turkey today, but at least he was my little turkey. Somehow that made it all seem worthwhile.

Toddler Tutorial 3: The Sound and the Fury

Toddlers are notorious for tantrums, those high-wattage emotional outbursts that usually erupt at the least convenient moment. Some kids seem to consider meltdowns a part of their daily schedule, while others explode only when life is piled high with more stimuli than their little psyches can handle.

Ferocious in their desire for control, toddlers simply can't process the fact that not all things in life will go their way. Even the most easygoing, compliant tots will occasionally let off steam in a dramatic fashion. My niece Zoe shocked my husband and me when she once had a bona fide tantrum right in front of us. It was nothing we hadn't seen before in our kiddies (actually, neither of Zoe's cousins had ever had so mild an outburst), but because she was for all accounts and purposes an angel, it was an amazing sight.

Rage Against the Machine

"Sometimes children become enraged. The primary way to tell when children are enraged is that they can no longer think rationally and their anger is now controlling them. Unfortunately, many parents try to talk their children out of anger, often leading to more intensity. The child who is enraged has lost control. You may see clenched fists, squinting eyes or a host of venting behaviors. Anger is one of those emotions that can grab you before you know what's happening. The intensity can build from frustration to anger to rage before anyone realizes it."   —Scott Turansky and Joanne Miller[1]

This astonishing display unfurled rather casually, beginning when my brother told Zoe it was time to go home. Apparently home-going was not on her agenda because she crumpled in a heap on the floor and just…lay there. Not too high on the Richter scale of tantrums seen around these parts, but there she was, not obeying her parents. The most acquiescent tot on the planet was getting in touch with her twenty-month-old angst, right there in front of us! She may have also glared a bit, and perhaps a tear or two was shed, but mainly she just folded like a deck of cards on the floor, lying in a heap and getting dog hair all over her cute outfit.

Well, we were floored, just floored. But it's true: Even angels have temper tantrums.

Toddler Unleashed

Listen to my pal Cheryl talk about her toddler's tantrums:

> Adrielle has a nice mixture of defiance and stubbornness going
> right now. She has a tendency to work herself into a froth over
> something—like wanting chocolate and/or suckers for every meal
> and snack—and being told no. My personal favorite is when she
> says something, and I totally cannot fathom what it is, so I take a
> guess at it. Usually I'm wrong, and then she will just go ballistic-
> psychotic and scream!
>
> Sometimes I'll offer her something and she'll scream, "No!"
> even if it's something I know she wants or needs (like a chocolate,
> a sucker, her blankie). She hits my hand away or takes the item and
> then flings it on the floor. When I take the flung item and put it
> on the table or in the kitchen or anyplace else, she'll scream again,
> demanding it back. She'll either take the item back and eat it or
> hold it—while looking at me in an extremely bitter way—or she'll
> fling-n-scream again. Makes for a nice day.

(Can I just say that this baby is absolutely angelic looking? She is.
Adopted from Korea as an infant, Adrielle looks like sugar and spice and
everything nice, yada-yada-yada. Just wanted to give you a little visual.)

It's easy to feel unhinged yourself during a tantrum, especially when
Baby Boffo pulls out all the stops and unleashes one of her famous triple-
decker scream/flail/snort numbers. But try to remember: Your job is to be
the grownup—calm, unflappable—the very bastion of solidity your toddler needs you to be right now.

Keep in mind that your child's outbursts are normal. Also, it may help
to know his tantrums are sometimes even cathartic. "Cries and outbursts
have a healing effect," says Aletha Solter, author of *Tears and Tantrums*.
"Children use them to resolve their feelings and release tension."[2] Just like

a good healthy cry can soothe your jangled nerves, so a screaming fit here and there can smooth over your little guy's rumpled emotions.

The key is to train your toddler to let off steam in appropriate settings, to calm herself, and to let you be her rock when she's out of control.

Meltdown Management

Head 'Em off at the Pass
The next time you sense the rumblings of an emotional explosion, try to employ that tool of tools: distraction. "Hey, look at the birdie in the tree!" or "Let's go find your new green dump truck!" or, my personal favorite, "Who wants a vitamin!" can sometimes divert and defuse a detonation. Sometimes.

Watch for Tantrum Triggers
You know this already, but a reminder never hurts: Your kid is more prone to meltdowns when she's hungry, tired, or sick. For Pete's sake, I feel a whole lot crankier when my blood sugar is dropping or I didn't get my required amount of beauty sleep. Throw a sore throat and pounding head into the picture, and I'm pretty much toast. Aren't you?

Keeping the kid well-fed and well-rested are two pounds of prevention right there. (And, yes, you are a slave to her naps!) When she's sick, try to keep your activities to a minimum if you can. Otherwise you're just asking for trouble.

Also, although it may seem obvious, many parents miss the fact that their little ones are stressed out not by taxes or a mean boss but by the things that vex their spirits. Toilet training can cause plenty of trepidation—and not just for you! Houseguests, even if they are Grandma and Grandpa loaded down with spoiling materials, can also be taxing for a toddler who is used to his usual routines and "roommates."

Another biggie is the addition of a new baby brother or sister. No matter how hard you may have tried to smooth your child's transition from Center of the Galaxy to Big Sister, the new baby can throw your older baby for a loop. Take Zoe, for example. Calm, sweet, agreeable Zoe. She was thrown for two loops when Mommy and Daddy came home with her twin brothers. When my brother Dan tried to change one of his twins on Zoe's changing table—she was twenty-two months at the time— she started screaming her head off. Yup, not only had Zoe's universe been bombarded with the flotsam and jetsam of two newborns, but now her daddy was placing one of the interlopers on her changing table! You can't blame Zoe for getting tense just as you can't blame your tot for coming unglued when the stuff of life seems piled higher than usual.

Sometimes the proverbial last straw is responsible for the howler. Zoe probably wasn't upset *simply* by the mere prospect of her brother using her changing table. In that case, it was more likely that the various letdowns and disappointments throughout the day had built up in volcanic fashion for my niece. Maybe Grandma didn't spend as much time playing with Zoe when she came to visit, and then Daddy reprimanded her for trying to drag one of her brothers off the couch. Mommy seemed to be glued at the breast with one or both of those pesky babies, and she didn't jump up and get Zoe the juice she asked for a very long time ago (ten minutes, but in toddler time, eons). Then all the people, coming and going, goo-gooing all over the twins. Enough already! So then the eensiest little thing—her property being appropriated by a seven-pounder—was just a pretext to let off some steam.

Teach Language That Liberates

By talking to and reading with your child every day, you teach him verbal skills, which in turn help him manage his emotions. Little ones who don't know how to put feelings to words perform them instead. So rather than say, "Give me…," they grab. Rather than say, "I'm mad at you," they hit or scream or kick or all of the above. Calmly say, "Use your words," or "Tell me what you want."

Be Their Shelter in the Storm

"If I'm dealing with an out-of-control, screaming, and can't-stop-it tantrum," says Cheryl, "what's generally worked for me is this: I pick the kid up, pin her little arms down, and hold her tight until the wiggling and squirming calms down. I usually sit or rock her and calmly say, "I've got you. You need to stop. I love you. You need to stop." Generally, she'll calm down, collapse in exhaustion, and sit on my lap quietly for a few minutes afterward. I'll hold her for a bit, feed her something, and try to get her into a new activity." Cheryl is absolutely right on target here. Holding your enraged little one can soothe him and provide him with a sense of security, or, if he's overstimulated by touch at this point, you can stand nearby and wait. Don't hover, though. Wash dishes or tidy up the room so as not to give him undue attention. Whatever you do, say as little as possible.

My Twenty-Four-Month-Old

"Petra is so funny when she has tantrums. It's all I can do not to laugh. (So far I've managed not to crack up while she's having a blowout!) She puffs out her chubby cheeks like a blowfish and narrows her eyes at me. Then she actually starts huffing and puffing, and I always expect to see smoke come out of her ears! When the screams start, though, it gets less funny and more annoying!"
—Angela

When Mount Olivia next erupts, your job is to comfort your banshee so she can regain some of that precious control. Tell her calmly that you understand she is very upset and that you will be there to help her when she is able to settle down.

Scott Turansky and Joanne Miller, founders of Effective Parenting Seminars, say this: "Whether it's the two-year-old temper tantrum or the fourteen-year-old ranting and raving, don't get sucked into dialog [during the tantrum]. It only escalates the problem. Talking about it is important, but wait until after the child has settled down."[3]

Whatever You Do, Don't You Lose It Too!

Sharon used to yell when her daughter, Lucy, had a meltdown. (As tempting as that can be, yelling plus yelling does not equal peace and quiet. The equation just makes things that much more volatile.) But now Sharon cuddles her little one and gently talks to her until the storm subsides. Supporting Lucy and giving in to her demands (for cookies, for Blue, or for dragging her open cup of grape juice around the house) are totally different things. Don't give in—or, as Winston Churchill said, "Never, never, never give in." Again, giving in just paves the way for histrionics every time something occurs that is not to the little diva's liking.

I admit that it does feel weird sometimes to be nice to your kid when he's acting like a whirling dervish. It feels more natural to punish, but that just means Mom's out of control too. It's important to show your toddler you love and support him, even if you are not going to buckle to his demands.

If Anyone Hates a Tantrum
More Than You, It's Him

When your child has his next fit, consider this: Your child actually hates going berserk and losing it because "it" (control) is what this whole thing was about in the first place! Being in control, having some say over his life—what to eat, wear, play with—is his mantra, his most fiercely guarded goal in life even if he doesn't have a clue.

Sometimes a toddler will stage a tantrum to try to get you to do what he wants. When this happens, it is probably because he feels he has no other recourse except to blow a gasket. His little brain is processing the following question: "If I scream and cry and kick, will Mommy give me that special toy in her room that prior to this moment I have not been allowed to play with? Hmmm." Don't give in. These little guys can wear a person down to a nub. I promise you, though, if you cave in this time, next time Hank wants to have a crack at your grandfather's antique toy car, it will be ten times harder to say no and have him believe you! To add insult to injury, because his motive was manipulative, Hank will probably feel even worse for having lost control. He knows he's being a shyster, and it feels bad! No matter what the scenario, when the histrionics subside, your child is likely to be exhausted and plenty unhappy with himself.

Cleaning Up the Aftermath

Some damage control is in order after a toddler's tempest. When you really, truly have not given in and the sniffles have subsided, try to get both of you on a fresh page. Resist the urge to blame, lecture, or punish. Instead, find something positive to say, like, "You did a good job calming yourself down today." Don't give in to his demands, but do give him a clean slate. Do something relaxing together, like taking a walk, reading a book, or baking. But don't give him attention above and beyond the norm, or he'll start to think tantrums are a good way to get attention.

As your toddler matures and can better handle his growing independence, the emotional lightning and thunder will ease off—if not completely, at least enough for you to catch your breath between episodes. Introduce a quiet activity such as coloring or reading, or pop in an upbeat video to transition from hysterical sobs and screams to the normal ruckus of life with a toddler. Normal is good. It shows little people that, yes, they were just sucked into a vortex of rage and despair, but somehow the world did not grind to a screeching halt. It only felt as if there were seismic shifts in the universe because, clearly, not much has changed. Life—hiccup—is actually not that bad after all.

Now, some likely scenarios and how to handle them:

Your two-year-old has his cousin over, but he yells blue murder whenever Cousin Callie reaches for his Winnie-the-Pooh.

Meltdown Manager: A two-year-old shouldn't realistically be expected to share a favorite toy. Before the playmate arrives, run interference and put away toys you know are cherished playthings. If he still goes berserk, gently but firmly remove him and explain he can join Callie again when he has calmed down.

Your twenty-three-month-old's voice is starting to get louder and more demanding. "Candy! I wanna candy!" she yells. You're grocery shopping and people are starting to stare.

Meltdown Manager Plan A: Whip out a granola bar or fruit juice snack that savvy you packed in your purse before leaving for the store.

Voices: Tantrum Tamers

"When one of our three kids had a toddler tantrum, we just stayed calm, partly ignoring their bad behavior and never letting on that it drove us nuts. This did let them vent their frustration over whatever they thought the injustice was. We intentionally let them vent because we didn't want to start any habits of stuffing emotions inside, which could eventually make their teenage years even harder for them. We have always told them, even when they were toddlers, that being angry is okay, as long as it's for the right reasons. We knew the logic behind our statement would not be comprehended for a long time, but we wanted them to hear the same story from us their whole life.

"When they saw that we were not negotiating and not reacting, they calmed down. There were times when we had to discipline for pitching a fit, and they soon realized that the consequence was going to happen and they still were not going to get their way. We have three kids, and each one responded differently: One caught on right away, another took a few tries, and the other still thinks she might get her way. Don't give up, and above all stay consistent with how

Plan B: She doesn't buy it. In fact, she seems more than just a little determined to get the green lollipop on display a mere five feet away. You know a meltdown's gonna come down. There's no way to prevent it. Remain calm. If you start yelling back, people are going to glare at you as if you're a mean mommy. Try to continue shopping, but make your way to the checkout. Steel yourself against the hysterics and say as calmly as possible, "I know you're angry right now, but you need to calm down." Some experts would say ditch the groceries where they are and leave the store, but I say that gives the kid way too much power. Abort a much-needed grocery run because of a tantrum? No way. Cut it short if you must, but continue as best you can. If you have to drag a bellowing two-

you decide to handle a tantrum or any bad behavior. Toddlers have an innate sense of justice, and when we don't dole out justice the same way every time for similar offenses, they will take the proverbial inch and go a mile."

—Linda

"When our first child was a baby, *Star Trek: The Next Generation* was in its Borg stage. So we started dealing with tantrums by stating in robotlike monotone: 'Tantrums are irrelevant.' The idea is that you simply weather the tantrum and then proceed exactly as you had planned. The tantrum does not earn the child anything. If you were going to give her a bath when the tantrum began, you still put her in the tub when it's over. This idea helped keep us from getting caught up in the hurricane of our little one's emotions. It also kept us from setting a pattern in which tantrums got some positive result. Eventually, we were able to discourage fussy fits with time-outs, but that only works once the child has some control over emotions."

—Debra

year-old out of the store, so be it. It's nothing your fellow shoppers haven't seen before, probably with their own toddlers. This way you'll still have some milk and bread in the fridge too.

How to Throw a Birthday Bash for a Two-Year-Old

1. A month before the big day, mull over your options. Should you throw a birthday party for your two-year-old? If so, should you invite family members, who populated Baby's first birthday, or her peers (she does seem to have a better social life than you)?

2. Decide to combine key relatives with a small, manageable peer group of guests. I read somewhere that the ideal number of guests should be one per year of the child, so choose two tots.

3. Fret about the fact that your rather high-strung neighbor Sally will have a cow if you don't invite her two-year-old, Norman III, to the party. Consider Norman's penchant for biting, scratching, and kicking—and wonder if you could have the party at an undisclosed location.

4. Be tugged from side to side as you consider the pros and cons of inviting Norman the Barbarian of Bertha Street to a party where the guest of honor actually dislikes him.

5. Cave in and put Norman on the list as you picture Sally having a cow. Vow to keep Norman under control.

6. Decide on a theme for the party. Elmo? Dora the Explorer? Butterflies? The list is truly endless. Your child seems to be on a cat kick lately so you decide on a cute kitten motif. Kittens it is!

7. Carefully plot a party time that will ensure a fresh and rested birthday child. Choose 3:00 P.M. so there's wiggle room in case your child takes a late nap.

8. Find kitten invites on the Internet and send them to grandmas, grandpas, aunts, uncles, cousins, plus of course, Ashlyn, Katelyn, and Norman *(grrr).*

9. Assemble goodie bags, prepare a Hello Kitty piñata, and plan age-appropriate games for the toddlers on the guest list.

10. Waffle between buying a cake at the bakery or rolling up your sleeves and actually baking the cake yourself.

11. Lean one way as you remember that time you made "cheese-cake" for your girlfriend's shower and everyone thought it was some kind of exotic custard.

12. Lean the other way as you think of how pleased your little girl would be with her very own homemade birthday cake. Become misty as you think about the cakes your own mother made for you. Picture the many Kodak moments that are sure to come when homemade goods are involved. Think, *How hard can it be?*

13. Reassess the value of producing home-baked goods when your from-scratch cake takes on the appearance of a massive chocolate pancake. Buy a box of cake mix and start over. Pain-stakingly follow directions in a cake decorating booklet and cut out cake cat ears. Ice your cake with chocolate icing, pipe in some feline facial features, drape some black licorice whis-kers, and call it good. Think, *Maybe I am a little bit domestic after all.*

14. On the day of the party, awaken an hour and a half early to your toddler's screams. The family Siamese has scratched her. Just a teeny "quit choking me" warning scratch, it's nevertheless enough to traumatize the child.

15. Hear the words, "I don't wike kitty." See the bottom lip jut out. Realize that your cat theme has gone down the tubes.

16. Greet guests with a cranky, napless toddler clamped onto your leg.

17. Grit teeth as your teenage brother-in-law says, "Hey! Cool beaver cake."

18. Assign teenage brother-in-law to Norman Patrol.

19. Grasp the fact that there are no "age-appropriate" games for two-year-olds.

20. Grasp the fact that people should never send two-year-olds to parties without diapers on them, even if they swear the kid is fully trained.

21. Grasp the fact that your teenage brother-in-law should not quit his day job at Krispy Kreme because he has failed miserably at being Norman's nanny.

22. Grasp the fact that Norman should never be given a stick to whack with, even if the intended target is a piñata.

23. Comfort Ashlyn and Katelyn as they recover from being whacked by Norman.

24. Forgo blowing out candles, in light of the fire hazard that is Norman, and cut the cake.

25. Restrain yourself when your teenage brother-in-law makes snide comment about the pink kitten paper plates. (Where did those piñata-whacking sticks go anyway?)

26. Thank the other mothers profusely for the kitten coin purse, the kitten Beanie, and the kitten book your daughter received for gifts and then promptly had no use for, in light of her anti-cat feelings.

27. Look at the birthday girl, fast asleep in the corner, where she was last seen playing with the ribbons and boxes her gifts came in.

28. Slump in an overstuffed chair and tell your husband he's doing the party when your child turns three.

Toy Story: Transitional Lovies and Fine-Motor-Skill Builders

Ryan is about to turn two, and her favorite plaything in all the world is her baby doll stroller. She pushes her baby doll around the house, the backyard, and even the neighborhood when she and her caregiver go for walks. Ryan's doll, a soft, floppy baby, is becoming more and more of a "transitional object." That is the technical term for a favorite doll, plush animal, or blanket that helps Ryan make the switch from being with you to being happily on her own. (More about dolls and play in the next chapter.) These kinds of "lovies" make wonderful birthday gifts for two-year-olds.

More hoots for your almost-two-year-old:

- *Simple jigsaw puzzles.* Your toddler may have the cranium power and fine-motor skills now to complete a super-simple, three- to six-piece jigsaw puzzle. Sturdy wooden tray puzzles with little knobs on each piece are the best. Tray puzzles help train the eye and develop the ability to match shapes. Experts say this skill primes the pump for when you tot begins to ID letters by their shapes.

- *More paper and crayons.* Ryan likes to try to copy her mommy's circles and lines. Though her circles look more like lopsided, cracked eggs, the time spent with her mom is valuable—and blissfully quiet. "When she actually draws something in the same ballpark as a circle, I tell her, 'Good job,'" says Ryan's mom, Sandy. "She just lights up and tries even harder."

- *Blocks for building towers.* See if your youngster can build a makeshift tower of six or more blocks. She'll probably want to smash her skyscraper, but prepare to be amazed at her progress from when you two first started to play with blocks.

- *Pop beads.* Twenty-three-month-olds can sometimes start to press pop beads together or string large wooden beads on a cord. Try this little activity and see if it's a go. If your tyke shows little interest, pick it up again in a few months when his fingers will be more dexterous and nimble (and his attention span is longer). Obviously, watch him like a hawk, especially if he's the type to put things in his mouth.

- *Sand, birdseed, and rice.* Any substance that is scoopable or pour-able offers opportunities to finesse her fingers and handwork. Squeezing moldable compounds like Play-Doh or cookie dough fine-tunes the same skills.

Fabulous Freebie: The Plastic Knife. "Right here is a good place to sing the praises of plastic picnic knives," says Allie Pleiter, author of *Becoming a Chief Home Officer.* "I am amazed at how much fun one toddler can have with a piece of celery and a plastic picnic knife. They're not sharp enough to cut little fingers, but you can saw away with amazing vigor at one of those things. And—voilà!—you have cooperative little cooks. Or at least cooks not reaching for the steak knives while you are trying to throw a chicken in the oven."[4]

Sweet Memories, Sibling Smackdown, and Social Graces for the Sandbox Set

You're halfway through the toddler years and well on your way to being the mother of a bona fide preschooler. Who knew it would race by so quickly? When my Ezra turned two, I took it hard, maybe because at the time we were unsure if we would have another baby. (But we are!) When your child turns two—or hits any birthday or milestone (such as starting preschool)—you have a great occasion to put pen to paper and reflect on the wonder of your growing child. By way of example, check out my own sappy, heartfelt letter to my two-year-old later in this chapter.

These months are prime for introducing doll play to your fun-time repertoire, so within these pages you'll read about the benefits of dolls for both (honest!) boys and girls. Also, since a toddler this age can really start to fight back when picked on by an older brother or sister, sibling smackdown starts in earnest. And speaking of smackdown, sharing toys or taking turns on the slide are still about as foreign to this age group as the food Vivienne ate in chapter 6. In Toddler Tutorial 4, learn how to guide your share-phobic tot to a life of give-and-take. It's not easy, but hey, someone's gotta do it!

Milemarker: A Regular Chatterbox

As your toddler's sense of himself as a separate person grows, he'll talk about himself—what he's doing, what he likes, and what he doesn't like. And when his language skills get legs, his imagination will be off and running. "Words are symbols—sounds that stand for objects and ideas. So when a child uses language, it's a sign she's able to think symbolically and imaginatively," says child development specialist Jay Cerio, Ph.D.[1] Your tot's memory is getting better, and he's beginning to understand abstract concepts such as "We're leaving soon" and "Granny is coming over later." Tomorrow doesn't make any sense yet, and neither does "three days" or "three months." Also, by your baby's two-year visit to the pediatrician, your child's preference for handedness will be clear. A righty or a lefty? For most tykes, it's now set in stone.

Hello, Dolly

Zoe's twin brothers are just three months old, so she spends quite a bit of time observing them getting fed. And fed. And fed some more. So in her inimitable toddler way, Zoe decided it was time to feed her own baby. She lifted her little shirt, hoisted her baby doll up to her chest, and started "nursing."

At two, Zoe is beginning to get that she's a separate person from her parents—and from her baby brothers, too. Playing with her doll helps her understand her relationship with her mom, her relationship with her dad, and their relationship to her and the twins. A doll is much more than just an inanimate plastic baby. Doll play is a sign of healthy psychological development. It gives toddlers a chance to process problems, learn social skills, exercise their vibrant imaginations, and even cultivate a love for learning. At this age, a tyke's new creative powers enormously affect how he interacts with dolls and stuffed animals.

Mothers of boys, stay tuned because—as you probably already know—

guys and dolls is no big whoop. Don't freak out if your burly boy's boy is choosing his sister's Groovy Girl over his monster truck. This is a completely normal and beneficial way for him to play. (I remember how my friend Bonnie's son, Tyler, now a big, strong defenseman on his peewee hockey team, loved to play with big sis Suzanne's dolls when he was two and three. Now that he's this strapping seven-year-old tough guy, he's all done with Barbie, Midge, and friends.)

Let me just underline this concept since, for whatever reason, it seems to unhinge some people to see their future man drag a doll around the house: Dolls are not a sign of effeminacy or an indication that your boy will grow up to be a drag queen or something. But in general, who knows why, boys are less interested in dolls than girls are. Another blanket statement: Girls often engage in doll play about mommies and daddies and

Voices: What a Doll!

"Josephine just started having a real interest in dolls over the last week or so. Her two dolls are Annie (Raggedy Ann) and a stuffed doll with two braids that she calls Baby Doll (a hand-me-down from her cousin Gracie). She will carry them around and sometimes ask me to 'take it' while her hands are busy with other things. I'm not quite sure how she relates to them, but she does give them big ol' kisses throughout the day. I'm not sure yet if she considers them little people like herself—but it's adorable to watch."

—Mary Jo

"Adam doesn't really play with dolls. He doesn't care much for stuffed animals in terms of cuddling. He has in the last month become really interested in faces. He has a 'learn to dress' type doll, and he is interested in the face (it is flat, his is not) and the yarn hair."

—Ann

sisters and cousins, while boys are more apt to create scenarios in which Batman is saving someone or punching the bad guy's lights out.

Sometimes, though, both boys and girls will figure out the same kinds of valuable things—autonomy, relationships, how people operate—with their stuffed animals. "Nathan loved stuffed animals, particularly dogs," says Laura. "He set them up for tea parties, birthday parties, and so on. One particular dog, appropriately named Travel Puppy, accompanied us on all overnight trips during the toddler years. Nathan 'fed' his stuffed animals, always in the kitchen, and generally considered them part of his own little family—whenever he wasn't preoccupied with trucks and trains, of course."

Both my sons displayed significant interest in dolls at one time or another. Ezra's personality is just more loving and cuddly than Jonah's, though, and he seemed to be more taken with the whole idea of " 'Arbies." One time I picked him up at the gym—he was probably twenty-eight months or so—and the nursery worker reported Ezra's fascination with a baby doll. "It was so cute," she said (and I agreed). "When I fed one of the [real] babies his bottle, Ezra pretended to feed the doll a bottle and then put it to bed."

Your son may never get into dolls, period, which means…nothing. Your daughter may never get into dolls either, which also adds up to a hill

Sleep, Baby, Sleep

Hopefully, your own sleep deprivation is a distant memory by now. Sleep is as important for your growing toddler as it was when he was a newborn, but now he'll probably resist it.

Ideally your two-year-old needs about eleven hours of sleep a night and one nap (one to two hours) during the day. Most munchkins this age go to bed sometime between 7:00 and 9:00 P.M. and get up between 6:30 and 8:00 A.M.

of beans. Whether a child picks up and plays with dolls or leaves them at the bottom of the toy box has a lot to do with individual personalities and quirks. "Ellie is a bit of a tomboy, so she really doesn't get into dolls that much," says my friend Jane. "When she does play, she's quite rough with them. She might say 'Mama, Baby crying' and then, 'Wham!' as she drops it on its head."

Just because Ellie is rough with her dolls doesn't mean she herself is treated roughly. Not at all! But sometimes doll play helps a toddler act out the ways he himself has been nurtured and disciplined. Experts say small children sometimes act very bossy with their dolls in order to work out in their minds how they are always told what to do and how to do it. When your sweetie sternly tells the doll "No!" or "Share!" she may be reenacting the power struggle she has with you and maybe even reinforcing a lesson you want to teach!

Dolls and stuffed animals can also boost a tot's sense of security when he's not with you. My friend Ana reports that her little one, Daniel, goes to bed at Grandma and Grandpa's much easier when he has his stuffed "ba." These special inanimate friends can also provide a new way for you and your child to play together. Your little one may dearly love to make you part of her story with the doll. Stuffed animals and dolls can smooth tough transitions such as good-byes and even biggies like new baby twins in the house. Mommy might say, "Good-bye, Raggedy Ann! I hope you and Kayla have fun together. We'll see you both when we get home." Or, "Zoe, I'm so glad you have Franklin to play with while Mommy takes care of the twins. You are a wonderful friend to Zoe, Franklin." Dolls are awesome!

Toddler Tutorial 4: Play Nice!

Let's review the Toddler's Creed:

> If I want it, it's mine.
> If I give it to you and change my mind later, it's mine.

If I can take it away from you, it's mine.

If I had it a little while ago, it's mine.

If it's mine, it will never belong to anyone else
no matter what.

If we are building something together, all the
pieces are mine.

If it looks like mine, it's mine.

If toddlers are infamous for one thing—other than chubby bellies, tantrums, and their adorable way of talking—it's their refusal to share. (This is why two-year-olds do not have timeshare condos.) "Who me? Willing to give up a piece of the action? I don't think so" is what they would say if they could. They would truly rather visit the dentist than give up a toy or a book or a piece of paper or a pinecone to another soul—especially another little soul. "What's mine is mine—don't touch it or you're toast—and what's yours is mine too, and the toast thing is still applicable." It's the died-in-the-wool manifesto of toddlers everywhere.

Yet somehow these incredibly egocentric members of the human race grow up to lend pens to coworkers, sugar to neighbors, and everything but their toothbrush to spouses (and sometimes they'll even do that!). How does this transformation from Nina the Narcissist to Socialized Adult come to pass? Unfortunately, it takes quite a bit of work on your part. And now is a pivotal time to get with the program. Already your tot's social life is probably better than yours, and she needs the skills to build on her natural inclination to enjoy other children.

While little ones should be reminded about taking turns and not seizing toys, the best way to ensure a smooth playdate is to provide toys for everyone. Amy, who has five young children ranging in age from two weeks to eight years, knows the drill when it comes to sharing. "Since Gabe, Maggie, Eva, and Malachi are spaced so closely together, sharing is probably our number-one discipline issue," she says. "I bought lots of duplicate toys so they could play side by side."

It's been interesting to watch Ezra and his cousin Zoe, who are both two, interact. They are always pleased to see each other, but they usually come to an impasse when one of them grabs a toy and even hides it so the other can't get his or her grubby paws on it. Both of them are much more willing to give and take with older kids, especially Jonah, in Zoe's case, for whom the sun rises and sets. (Ez loves his big brother, but since they live in the same house, all bets are off when it comes to sharing. Put plainly, Ez just wants anything and everything Jonah has in his possession and will go to great lengths to obtain an item for himself, resulting in combat. But I digress.) Plus, as far as Zoe can tell, her big cousin Jonah is not all that interested in two-year-old toys anyway. Toddlers can almost smell a rival for their playthings, and if their opponent is lurking nearby, they will definitely be on edge. So let me offer some ways to take the edge off what would otherwise be a wonderful social time.

Protect the Good Stuff

"To help calm Amber down when playmates came to visit," says Erin, "we permitted her to set aside one or two special toys that she didn't want to

Well, That's No Fun

When a young mom complained to Vicki Iovine about a woman in her playgroup who would yell at any child in conflict with her own eighteen-month-old, Iovine responded, "Whatever you do, don't leave the playgroup in a huff. I think I would have lost my mind while I was raising three kids under the age of four if I didn't have a chance to meet and chat with other mothers. Make the group work for you." She suggested the playgroup appoint a leader who could deal with such matters and hammer out some rules and procedures for dealing with conflict resolution between kids or etiquette between moms.[2]

share. Of course, she couldn't play with them while her friends were over, but she seemed comforted by this protection of her favorite toys and more willing to share others."

Give Them Words

By now your toddlers may have the verbal skills in place for you to teach him some "share talk." Instead of the old "screech and snatch" routine, tutor your little one to say, "I want the truck, please." This will help him express his true intentions and desires, cutting down on the slapping and grabbing that sometimes accompany this interaction.

Here's another use-your-words tip from the toddler trenches: "Instead of telling Ethan to share, we've taught him to say 'done' when he's finished playing with a toy," says Frank, Ethan's dad. "Then his friend or his brother can play with it. The other kids catch on and say 'done' as well, and they don't seem to even mind sharing that much when they know they'll get another turn."

Use a Timer

Buy a little egg timer, maybe one with a fun motif, and use it to referee squabbles. Bridget uses this idea with her daughter Charlotte: "When Charlotte has her friend Danica over, they usually end up in a tiff over one of the dolls," she says. "I have learned to set an egg timer for two minutes and tell the girls when the buzzer goes off, it's time to take turns. Because it's the egg timer that is telling them what to do—that is, share—I get a lot less grief from Charlotte. Plus, the girls seem to enjoy the novelty of the egg timer and the idea that until the buzzer goes off, the much-coveted dolly is all theirs." Brilliant!

When All Else Fails

Take the golden plaything away so that no one can see it or play with it. This drastic measure usually results in whining—at least—and screaming hissy fits at worst. Stick to your guns, though. Maybe next time the little tyrants will get the clue that battling over a toy is a good way to see it disappear.

Social Graces for the Playground Pals

One arena for many toddler skirmishes is the playground. Just as your little darling has a bit of trouble handing over her toy teapot, she's also apt to loathe sharing the playground apparatus. Because the park is a satellite location for you—meaning it's not your home—you may have to plan a little more to make for smooth sliding and swell swinging.

- *Bring extras.* Throw a few extra shovels, pails, and whatnots into your bag, or at least bring more than only your child's favorite toy on the planet. If you don't, you're asking for a sandbox scuffle. Bring an extra juice box or cheese stick, too, so no fights will erupt over snacks. Naturally, ask the other child's mom or dad or babysitter if he can have whatever you're doling out. (There's always a child at the playground with no adult supervision, or very little anyway. Model kindness by sharing your snacks with these kids.)

- *Ask permission.* If you find a toy that's not being used by its owner, allow your child to play with it. Obviously, though, if the owner is right there, ask his parent or caregiver and get your toddler to say thank you. If the other child wants her plastic shovel or whatever back before your child is done, try to move on to another activity, such as sliding.

- *Keep watch.* It's always a sticky wicket to discipline another child when his parent is sitting right there. But kids can be rough, and you want to make sure your child and others are safe. If a pintsized bully is pushing or grabbing stuff or throwing sand (the worst!), give his caregiver a chance to intervene. If she just sits there and continues to read her magazine, ignoring the fact that her child is being a brat, step in and give a firm but gentle directive to the offending child: "No throwing sand, please."

- *Forewarn your departure.* As I've mentioned, toddlers hate to be pried away from an incredibly fun activity such as swinging. Give your swinging girl a heads-up a few minutes before it's time to go, and she may leave her beloved park and playmates with less fuss.

Step Out of the Ring, Mom!

There's nothing worse than competitive mothering, and sometimes the toddler years can bring that out in moms. Maybe it's because there are so many behavioral challenges in parenting a toddler, but somehow parents seem to be quite defensive about their two-year-olds. Or really, their precious offspring at any age! My friend Sabine relates this frustrating moment with her friend, whom we will call "Mary."

Mary is always so calm with her kids, it's almost unnerving. But I have to remind myself that her kids are very, very calm and compliant. Her daughter Lauren, who is about two now, will sit for hours, literally, on Mary's lap and not say a word. If that were my Holden, he would have been going through the garbage and scooping dirt out of the plant holders!

One time Mary watched Holden for a few hours, and he was his usual rambunctious self. They have a phone sitting on the couch arm—right there in plain view and accessibility to their two small children! Well, Holden of course went right for it and tried to dial Taiwan a few times before Mary intercepted the phone and put it somewhere he couldn't get to it. When I got back she said, "You know, it's the funniest thing. Lauren and Breanne have never once even touched the phone, and Holden made a beeline for it." I was like, "Well, duh!"

I honestly think my two boys have way different personalities than Mary's girls. I don't think the difference is because I'm not as effective a parent as she is, but sometimes she makes me feel that

"I'm Too Old"—a Letter to Ezra
on the Occasion
of His Second Birthday

My beautiful boy,

Can you really be two years old? (When I asked you how old you were, you held up two fingers and said, "I'm too old.") I admit it, Ez, it's hard for your silly mom to let go of her baby. So it's a good thing that in so many ways, you are still babyish. You still wear footie pajamas (about half the time, anyway). You still have that luscious baby smell sometimes, *eau de bebe,* with a base of apple juice and baby shampoo, plus hints of other stuff, like crayons and Dinah, our dog. Above all, you still love to snuggle with me, Daddy, and "Bama" (which goes for either Grandpa Pat or Grandpa Craker, not to mention Oma). Your "love language" is definitely touch.

But the boy is fast emerging now, and as much as I want to keep my baby, I do thrill at the little guy you've become.

Just the other day you were looking at a book, and you said, "Puh-pull," correctly identifying the color purple. I went around all day long, bragging to people that you could tell purple from blue! You love to name your colors, and you are brilliant at it, if I do say so myself. You also talk quite a bit, too. "I want mo juice," "I want Jonah," or "Mommy no sing!" are some frequent sentences you utter.

A few days ago, we were in Ile des Chenes, Manitoba, at Tyler Anderson's hockey game. I thought you might be bored, standing in a cold arena with no place to run and no toys to play with. But instead, when the game ended, we had to drag you out of there, kicking and screaming, "I want to play hockey!" My mother's heart swelled with pride over that, of course.

(continued)

You adore horses, and I imagine you will play with plastic horsy figures for ages. Maybe you will be Grandpa's long-awaited cowboy! Dinosaurs, doggies, kitties—you love 'em all! And books, too. While most of the time you are more wiggly, busy, and wild than most any other tots I've encountered, you will sit at the drop of a hat to flip through a book. Currently you enjoy books about rabbits most of all, and nightly we read you a couple of your bunny stories. Also, Dr. Seuss's classic *One Fish, Two Fish, Red Fish, Blue Fish,* a Christmas present from us, is going over extremely well.

You are becoming quite the playmate for Jonah. As long as you keep your paws off his Bionicle (or whatever sacred toy), he's quite happy to play with you. You follow him everywhere and repeat every word out of his mouth. Of course brotherhood is a classic double-edged sword. You two fight like a couple of growling puppies with their teeth on the same chew toy. Still, for you, the sun rises and sets on your big brother.

As of today, Ezra, you're also a big cousin. Your twin cousins Jadon and Eli were born this morning, strapping seven-pounders, happily in vibrant good health. I know you will be a friend and role model for them, just as your big cousins—Michael, Jake, and Ryan—are for you. (This Christmas you enormously enjoyed every moment in the company of Michael and Jake, who teased you and played with you and generally showered you with attention.)

Your answer to everything is "No!"

"Were you a good boy at the gym?"

"No!"

"Are you Mommy's fluffhead?"

"No!"

"Do you want a piece of candy?"

"No!" And then a few seconds later, "Canny pease!"

It's as if you want to determine your own destiny as well as exert your independence every chance you get, if only for a moment of control. You're obstinate, passionate, emotional, and getting you to do something you'd rather not (like get dressed when Elmo is on), takes United Nations levels of diplomacy. I hope we can shape your will, not break it, and help you become a strong man of God. I hope you are always knit close to my heart, and to your dad's, and to your heavenly Father.

Love always,
Mommy

way. She doesn't understand why I need breaks from my kids, time to recharge my batteries. Apparently Mary's batteries never need recharging! I love her and think she's a great mom, but I wish sometimes she had even an inkling of what my life chasing two boisterous kids is like and could be more understanding. To be honest—and I'm ashamed to admit this—but she's pregnant right now with a boy, and I'm kind of secretly hoping he gives her a run for her money!

Comparing kids is easy to do, but try not to. Instead keep in mind that every child is different and has a different set of gifts and struggles. If Sabine and Mary are going to be spending loads of time together, Sabine might work up the nerve to say something to Mary about adopting a more balanced view, something like, "Every child is different and has a different set of gifts and struggles." I know I caught myself recently with a comment I made to my friend Tamara. Her daughters are mellow and don't appear to give her much trouble at all. "That's not motherhood," I said, jokingly referring to how her angels respond so well to her every command. Later I thought, *Why did I say that?* Of course Tamara is experiencing motherhood! She's still up at night with the ear infections and packing lunches and changing diapers. She just doesn't have to deal with my particular challenge of having strong-willed, active boys. She might have to deal with shyness or maybe a lack of drive or possibly kids who might be followers instead of leaders just by their more laid-back personalities. And then again, she might not!

I remember one mom of an eight-year-old complaining that her child wanted to stay in her room and read books 24/7, summertime included. Now, some days that scenario sounds appealing, but it actually was a big problem for her because she had to constantly try to get her daughter to socialize, exercise, or just about anything that didn't involve reading in her room. The point is, we all have to keep in mind the fact that each and every mother faces different struggles—and different rewards.

Toy Story: Spark the Imagination

When my Ez turned two, I felt that strange mingling of exultation that my baby was growing and developing and becoming his own little person—and genuine sorrow that my baby was, well, growing and developing and becoming his own little person. Wasn't it yesterday he would sleep in my arms, a snuggly bundle in his butter-yellow footie pj's? Sigh. It's that paradox of motherhood, that necessary pushing them out into the world, yet pulling them back for nurturing and love. So it's kind of cool that toddlers at this age are still operating under their own push/pull M.O. Even though Ez had become increasingly independent over the preceding twelve months, he still needed me at close range, a mobile satellite station always nearby for a love-tank refuel.

This need for mom to be here/need for mom to be elsewhere is evident in new twobies as they play. Ez wanted me to show him how to match pictures in his chunky picture lotto game, yet no sooner than I would be getting smoked in the game then he would say, "Bye, Mama!" (They say these matching games are great for foundational math skills, but I found that the scattered pieces became more of a nuisance than anything. Plus, at this age—and for three more years unless you've got an extraordinarily compliant child—kiddies make up their own rules. But hey—it can't hurt, right? Maybe all this sorting of Bob the Builder and

✦ Faith Builder

To ingrain in your toddler that the Bible is set apart from other books, approach it differently. Talk about how God's Word is special, and pray and ask God to help you and your tot to understand what you read.[3] "From infancy you have known the holy Scriptures, which are able to make you wise for salvation through faith in Christ Jesus" (2 Timothy 3:15).

Wendy pictures will lead to a brilliant career in math. Maybe my savant sorter will laugh all the way to calculus club one day in the future. Right now, though, I'm too busy craning my neck under furniture, trying to find that long-gone Spud picture.)

My Twenty-Five-Month-Old

"Bennett *loves* to tease, to grab something from Max and run away with it. One time he spotted something Max had placed on the floor momentarily, and—like a hawk swooping down to get that mouse—he grabbed it and ran down the hall. He didn't miss a beat! He was *real* smooth, and it almost went unnoticed. And all this just to get a reaction out of Max!"

—Alanna

Imaginary play is superb for middle-aged toddlers. Playing "doctor" with a doll, spooning "medicine" into her little mouth and checking her ears can easily lead to solo play as toddlers get wrapped up in the scenario they are creating in their minds. Same with cars and trucks. Mom or Dad or Granny or whoever can initiate a grand game of "car wash" and then be amazed at how their half-pint pump jockey will start chattering away to himself, reenacting the real-life swabbing of the family minivan that took place two days before.

Obviously, toy car washes and gas stations are great launching pads for imaginary play, being as they are miniversions of familiar, day-to-day operations. Here's some other cool stuff to turn your two-year-old's creative-thinking crank:

- *Toy kitchens, plastic dishes, and picnic, baking, or grocery-shopping sets.*
- *Garage-sale finds for dress-up adventures.* Sunglasses, sparkly shoes, hats, gloves, purses, vests, tutus—there's no end to the possibilities.

- *Toys that make real-life sounds, such as telephones that ring or dolls that talk.* For Ez, his talking Larry the Cucumber and Bob the Tomato hold endless fascination. As he whacks their soft bottoms on a hard surface, Ez listens intently to Larry Boy insisting—for the seventy-fifth time—that he is not a pickle.
- *Large transportation toys with buttons to make a horn honk or a siren whistle.* Those huge plastic ride-on vehicles and tricycles are stellar for building leg muscles and coordination. (But not the $300 motorized ones. Huh-uh! Those just scream, "I am spoiled beyond all reason." Plus, for much, much less cash, you can get a "car" that's powered by a kid's own feet, a la Fred Flintstone—the way God intended!) Scope out garage sales for this goody, because they are as durable as Barney Rubble's own coupe and will last forever—or at least until your Bam Bam gets a real driver's license. Ours was purchased for $25 at a garage sale when Jonah was eighteen months old, and it has lasted through two kids—and counting.

Fabulous Freebie: Sand. There's a reason why sandboxes are standard issue at playgrounds all over the planet. Sand has all sorts of mesmerizing qualities, and playing in it can boost dexterity like crazy. Your little sandman will be transfixed by its stickiness when he dumps water on it and by how it can get gritty when he pats it down with his hands. Fill up buckets, dump 'em out. Repeat seventeen times. Scoop and dig and pat and mound and scrape and sweep—you don't even need sand toys, although they do make things a bit more fun. At the beach, watch out for deceased fish and other creatures that have seen fresher days. At the playground, check for garbage such as—I hate to say it—condoms and cigarette butts. Hey, it happens, and the last thing you need is for Curious George to grab one of those. In your yard, remember to cover your sandbox with a plastic sheet or a lid so that Fluffy next door doesn't think of it as her own private outhouse.

Sweetness, Suffering (from Whining), and One Stubborn, Stubborn Boy

One of the chief compensations your toddler offers for his often maddening and fractious ways is his great love for you and your mate, not to mention Grandma, Grandpa, Auntie Rachel, and Uncle Jeff. For all their personality "quirks," toddlers more than make up for it all with their great big, boisterous hearts. This chapter contains one of my favorite sections—about love and your growing baby, although he's not such a baby anymore, is he? He's definitely old enough to have perfected the art of whining. If toddlers are famous for love, they are also notorious for making that obnoxious whimpering noise known to have made the most serene mother come unglued. In Toddler Tutorial 5 we'll delve into some tested tips for dealing with the little whiner in your life. Finally, I have for you another installment of the "Life with Ez" chronicle. Be a fly on the wall at my house as I continue to ponder the mysteries of perhaps the world's most stubborn—and sweet, I must say—toddler. God knew we needed these tiny people to be so stinkin' cute and sweet to balance out the other stuff!

Milemarker: A Firm Word Takes the Heat Off

"No!" "NO! *"NO!"* Tired of repeating the word *no* all the time like some kind of warped CD? Your newly-minted two-year-old will take every opportunity to test your limits. As we've already covered thoroughly, you know she's not being a tyrant merely for the sake of being a tyrant. She's just following her inner muse to exert her own independence. "Indeed, it is through your child's exploration and struggles, often with you," says Baby Whisperer Tracy Hogg, "that your toddler begins to gain mastery over her environment and, most important, gains a sense of herself as a

Voices: How My Toddler Shows Love

"Willow is a hugger. She will come up when we least expect it and tackle any of us with a nice tight squeeze. She climbs up on our laps and snuggles in with bottle in hand. Because her sisters are seven, twelve, and fourteen, they've been her caretakers as much as Mom and Dad—so when she needs comforting, she will just as easily go to one of her sisters as to us. Sometimes she prefers them, which I don't always like, but I'm glad she's close to her sisters. They adore her."

—Traci

"Toddlers are delightfully loving. Our son, Nathan, has always been wonderful at sharing. (We'll see how that changes with the arrival of a sibling!) As a toddler he particularly enjoyed sharing food and would become upset if we said 'no, thank you' to one of his soggy Cheerios. 'But I'm just sharing!' he'd exclaim in exasperation. He also loved (still does) to snuggle in bed with us in the mornings—mostly on Mama's side 'cause Daddy's just a bit grumpy first thing. He'd bring his stuffed animals in to share with us too."

—Laura

competent and independent being."[1] You can take the heat out of exasperating moments by explaining the reasoning behind your rules. Saying "You have to sit in your car seat so you'll be safe" will make it easier for her to agree.

"I Love You"

Toddlers have a rap sheet a mile long—and rightfully so. But these vexatious little people also have one big compensation: They are full of love for their mommies and daddies. Their little hearts are brimming over with

"Ellie is very stingy with her affection. She definitely has to be 'in the mood' or you'll get nothing of her. She will once in a while do a 'butterfly kisses, doggy kisses, daddy-daughter kisses' routine with Jamie. I feel most loved by her when I pick her up from nursery or come home after going out and she runs up saying 'Mama!' exuberantly, combined with a huge grin and tight hug. She does the same for Jamie."

—Jane

"Oh, the land of sweet baby kisses! I don't have the exact date written down, but at about a year I taught Adam to give kisses. I would say, 'Can Mommy have a kiss?' and make kissy noises at him, and then he'd come over, lean in, and give me a kiss. Sometimes it is a sweet tender baby kiss that feels like the wings of a butterfly, and other times it is a full open-mouth slobber. If Adam is too busy to give a kiss, he will lean his forehead into mine in a gentle head butt and allow me to kiss him."

—Ann

affection and tenderness for the ones who cherish them. And we can't help but respond in kind. When a small child who holds your heart cups your face with his chubby little fingers, you dissolve into a puddle. Or when the little girl you treasure more than life itself snuggles into your lap and nestles her soft curls into your neck—life is as sweet as it gets.

Recently Doyle and I took Ezra to see Barney live and in...person...or whatever. The tots in attendance were crazy for him, their tiny faces alight with wonder and joy and adoration. I'm convinced the reason they love the purple dinosaur so much is because he is so unabashedly sappy. Sure, you and I go into sugar shock after a few minutes of watching Barney skip and wave and giggle, but our toddlers are glued to the image on the screen, that great big purple lump of lovin'.

I interviewed (ahem) Barney over the phone not long ago so I could write a preview story for his upcoming show in Grand Rapids. He was, of course, "in character." At the end of the interview, I asked if he would be willing to say hi to my two-year-old. Wide-eyed and wonder-filled, Ezra was overjoyed. (Yet it seemed absolutely normal to him that Barney would be on the phone.) "I love you, Barney," Ezra said, grinning from ear to ear. The conversation was short—naturally, a blue-chip celeb like Barney can't spend all day having his fans slobber all over him—but sweet, the gist being that Ez loved Barney and Barney loved Ez.

Toddlers lavish the ones they love with the sweetest parts of their hearts and souls. Sometimes when I am at the end of my rope with Ez— and I'm telling you that rope is nothing more than a frizzled piece of twine by that time—he tries in his own unflagging way to reestablish the love connection. "Mommy, you so piiiiiitty," he'll say, head cocked to the side, cheeks dimpling, blue eyes twinkling. Or my favorite: "Mommy, you a pin-cess." The little bugger! The sad part is, his approach usually works. Why? Because I know this child sincerely adores me with all the emotion and expanse of his spirit. And when he's been rough on me, he can sense it, and suddenly he wants to be Mommy's sweetheart once more.

Experts speak of the limbic brain, the layer of the brain which is the abode of all emotion. It's there that we—and our toddlers—cry and fear and giggle, where our hearts are pierced by the thought of something bad happening, and where they melt when we hold our little ones in our arms. "Love lives in the limbic brain," says writer Lauren Slater. "Through touch and talk and movement, we're able to shape, in ways perhaps more profound than we imagined, the orb between our child's ears."[2]

 ## My Twenty-Six-Month-Old (or a Mini "Life with Ez")

One morning when I was doing the dishes, Ezra started crying. I looked over, and to my absolute horror, he had glued his eye shut with my nail glue. It was one of those moments when time and space just stand still. Instantly I recreated the crime: Ez had supposed that my nail glue was eye drops, being a similarly shaped bottle and, copying me, had dropped some glue in his eye. Mercy me! I was a mess, imagining emergency rooms and irreversibly damaged eyesight! I quickly washed his eye with a warm washcloth. Thankfully, the glue had not yet set, and I was able to pry his eyelids open. Thank God!

Science affirms that touching and caring boosts brain cells and overall health. Rocking a child in comfort, squeezing him in a hug, stroking his little red-apple cheeks, rubbing his back—all this is bundled in the limbic brain's memory. And these limbic love notes will stand him in good stead for the rest of his life. You are your toddler's first and primary teacher when it comes to love, and—over the course of thousands of cuddles and hand holds and forehead kisses—"the neural messages become engraved, much the same way shells bear the swirls of the sea," says Slater.

So the next time your angel throws herself into your arms, lights up like the Fourth of July at the sight of you, or whispers, "I wub you,

Mama," know that you have taught her well and that your lessons have come back in manifold rewards.

Toddler Tutorial 5: The Days of Whine and "No-ses"

Sometimes those loving moments of sweetness can seem few and far between. "I sometimes feel like my two-year-old Ava's in control around here," says mom Wendy. "I usually don't back down on the no and let her walk all over me, but whining really wears me down! I feel like I never get any time to relax. I'm always chasing her, keeping her out of trouble, cleaning up her messes. I love Ava and I enjoy being her mommy, but sometimes it's like she knows if she whines louder, she'll get what she wants!"

Does anything mash one's nerves to smithereens more than the sound of whining (from a person whose boogers you have just removed)? Truly, I'd sometimes rather be in a cage full of wild beasts than cooped up in a house with a bunch of short, whimpering people mewling in a tone so piercing, surely the neighbor's dog has picked up on it.

And toddlers are whiners par excellence! By the time they reach two, most rug rats have mastered that loud, cranky, increasingly higher-pitched demand for chips that will make that bag of Doritos pop right open. It's enough to make a grown woman cry—or whine herself—right there in the checkout line.

When I ask moms of toddlers what their child's biggest behavioral issue is, more often than not they say it's whining. I myself would prefer a tantrum or even a public meltdown over having to deal with a fussy little boy who doesn't seem to quite know what it is he wants. Actually, that's a key point: Toddlers don't know what they want, and even if they do, they don't have the communication skills to tell us. Frustrated, they start whining. Plus, our kids have it on good authority that a certain insufferable, needling, shrill tone of voice gets results. That's all they want—results, whether it be nachos, candy, ice cream, a toy, juice, a television show, or even a cuddle with Mom who's been on the phone half the day. (Sometimes a whimpering kid just needs someone she loves to get down to eye level with her for a genuine connection.) But unless you want your whiner to gain complete control of you and all your emotional assets, it's vital to teach him new and improved ways of getting his points across to those who care for him.

For those days, though, when the whining is getting under your skin, to follow are seven Whine Busters from the toddler trenches.

1. Call Her on the Carpet

Think little Miss Snivels knows how annoying her voice is? Actually, she hasn't got a clue. Call a whimper a whimper (for example, "That's a whiny voice you're using"), and if she doesn't get it, do a demo for her. For comic relief, exaggerate really horrid whining and then a really pleasant voice.

2. Remove the Culprit for the Benefit of Nonwhining Society

"I may be on to something that gets our two-year-old's attention," says Joanne. "For the past few weeks, when Aidan starts to get wound up and whines, we call his name to establish eye contact. When we know we have Aidan's attention, we say in a firm voice, 'Stop that whining. If you don't stop whining, you will go to your room.' Then we wait to see if he keeps whining. The first time he disobeys again, we pick him up and take him to his room. We don't shut the door, but we put Aidan on the bed and explain that when he stops whining, he can come out and play. The first time we tried this, I wasn't at all sure he really understood what was going on, but after about four separate tries over the last week, I think this method actually works pretty well. Usually Aidan cuts out his naughty behavior within five minutes and comes out of his room. Yesterday he was whining up a storm, and I put him on his bed and gave him the little speech about being able to join us for lunch when he was done whining. Before I even left the room, he had stopped whining, and we all had a very nice, whine-free lunch!"

3. Reward the "Big Girl" Voice

Whenever your child asks for something in an affable way, try to give her what she needs as promptly as you can. This clues the savvy tot into the fact that pleasant voices get results, action, good things, while fussiness gets nada. If you can't do what she wants right then and there, take a second to acknowledge her need, give her a ballpark estimate for when you'll respond ("Honey, I know you want more juice. Hang on two minutes, and I'll get it"), and follow through.

4. Teach Him the Words That Express the Problem

If your child can't get past the whining, try restating the issue for him. For instance, say, "I can see that you're not happy. Is it because I can't read a story to you right now?" This modeling will enable you to get a dialogue going.

5. Try the "Three Strikes and She's Outta There!" Approach

"When my daughter whines, we have a three-step approach," says my friend Linda. "We initially respond with a pleasant 'When my big girl Georgia comes back and the whiny-voiced girl who took her place goes away, then Momma will talk about this.' When that doesn't work, then I move to step two, with a firm, now-I-mean-it voice: 'I will not speak to a child who whines. When you can talk like the big child you are, then I will speak to you again.'" Step three is the time-out. We have threatened other disciplines she fears more, but haven't had to follow through because she knows we are serious about using the time-out, so she knows we are serious about using those options if need be."

6. Be Steadfast

No matter whether your toddler wants a juice refill or wants to dump the sugar bowl on the floor (and then lick it up), you need to make him understand that his way of asking is not an option. Sometimes I just say, "Say it nicely," to Ezra and he changes his tune. Or try sending a visual message by holding your hands over your ears and rolling your eyes in mock pain to signal that you hear whining. (Cup your ears and smile serenely when you don't.) Most important—and this is so hard—don't cave in if you can possibly stand it. As I've mentioned, being perverse creatures, toddlers will recall your one collapse and evermore push to see if you'll fall apart again.

7. Plan to Stay Cool in Combat

It's so much easier to cave in when all the eyes in the grocery store are on you (at least it sure feels as though everyone is looking). The last thing you want your toddler to figure out is that whining in public is an effective way to get what he wants, so stick to your guns. No matter where you are or who you're with or what kind of tone your toddler uses, don't buckle.

Envision the following scenario played out at the store: Munchkin begins to whimper that he wants Sugarpalooza candy. You shake your head no and continue shopping. Munchkin intensifies his tone, ratcheting it up a few notches until it starts to bore a hole in your cranium. You say no again and continue shopping. At the checkout counter, the woman in front of you has seven hundred items in her cart. Munchkin sees his golden opportunity and combines the whine with a gutteral crying-type noise that is simply insufferable. White-knuckled, teeth gritted, jaw clenched, you grip your cart handles and stare at the tabloid photo of an alien family from Jupiter, trying desperately to ignore your toddler. You wonder if this alien family would like to adopt your child. Munchkin keeps it up, way up. You pay for your items, dash out to the minivan, and race home. Munchkin sits slumped in his car seat, defeated and morose. The sound of a thousand mosquitoes buzzing in your ear has ceased. You have won the day!

Life with Ez: Tomorrow Will Be a Better Day

My boy has a will of iron ore. According to some kind of fine-tuned timing system known only to him, he refuses to do my bidding no matter how sweetly and persuasively I coax him.

One of his favorite mulish behaviors is dropping to his knees in the middle of the street, usually in deep snow or a mud puddle, and never with protective snow/rain gear on his chubby little knees. We can be having a delightful afternoon, a fuss-free time of jokes and silliness—all is sunshine. Then, without warning, the little shyster will just drop as if seized by a sudden urge to feel snow or rain through his (clean) pants.

"Get up, Ez," I'll say, quite calmly at first.

"No!"

"C'mon now, you have to get up. Your pants are getting wet and cold."

"No!"

"Ez-ra, I said get up out of that puddle now! You obey Mommy!"

"Har-umphhhh."

And there he sits, huffing and puffing, not moving a micromillimeter.

And there I stand, huffing and puffing, trying to fill my lungs with those nice, soothing deep breaths they talk about in anger-management articles. Sooner or later a vehicle will make its way down the street, and the stalemate is broken by my heaving the little donkey up off the ground and wrestling him into his car seat.

But give me a power struggle in broad daylight any day of the week over the worst of the worst: middle-of-the-night clashes. Take last night, for example. Ez woke up crying about four times. I stumbled out of bed and covered him or gave him a drink or whatever, until I got it through my fuzzy, REM-deprived cerebrum that the kid probably had an ear infection.

Arrrgh! Apparently that ten-day run of amoxicillin we just went through didn't work. Which meant more sleepless nights. And a doctor's appointment to be fit in where exactly? And more pink stuff. Spoonfuls and spoonfuls of that ever-lovin' pink stuff.

Deep sigh. Well, nothing could be done right then and there except to tromp all the way downstairs and grab a teaspoon and some kiddie pain reliever. I'd give him a dose of Tylenol, and with any luck we wouldn't hear a peep until morning.

 ## Hey, Whatever Works

"Bennett had been sleeping wonderfully for many months, but he recently started waking up at night, mad. I'd try to soothe or comfort him, and he would get ticked. I'd pick him up to take him for a drink of milk, and he'd get ticked. I'd try to rock him, and he's ticked. Massage his foot that he claimed was hurting—ticked. One time we even clipped his toenails in the middle of the night, thinking they were hooking on his socks. Another night we made him eat a banana because we thought hunger might be the problem. Craziness, eh? I'm chuckling even as I write this. I told my mom about this, and she gave me something to think about. *Maybe he needs to go pee in the potty.* Well, I thought, it wouldn't hurt to try. I don't always heed my mom's fifties and sixties childcare methods (like feeding babies cereal at two months old or having them potty trained by eighteen months), but this time I took her advice. Guess what? He is sleeping much better! He wakes up like clockwork at 12:30 A.M. with his diaper a little wet, if not completely dry. I lead him to the potty, and he pees into it. Now that we're in this routine, instead of rousing five or six times, he's only rousing once or twice."

—Alanna

Except for one tiny little detail.

My intractable baby boy decided he didn't want medicine at that moment. (Usually he's a great trooper for medicine. He'll accept a spoonful of anything remotely fruit-flavored.)

"No!" he yelled and thrashed around when I moved in with the spoon. I asked nicely, sweetly even. Then I became more commanding. Finally I stooped to the lowest of the low—the juice-in-a-bottle bribe. (You dentists are recoiling in horror, I'm sure, but believe me, the specter of tooth decay at that moment was very dim indeed compared to the importance of getting my weary bones back in bed. I would have given the kid a bucket of sugar at that point had he only opened his mouth.)

"As soon as you take the medicine, you can have juice in your ba!"

Well, even this irresistible and limited-time-only offer made no dent in the brick wall.

"Whaaaaghaffffttt!!!!" His wails were now muffled in his pillow as he flipped over onto his stomach. Why in Sam Hill wouldn't he take the medicine? He knew that it wasn't gross and that medicine usually means his ouchies go away! This was driving me crazy, the contrariness of it all. If he had just opened his trap the first time I asked, he could have already been feeling better, and I could have been falling back to sleep instead of arguing with a thirty-pound person (and losing) at four in the morning!

It was time for Mommy to pull out the big guns—or stand there all night with a spoon in her hand.

"Ezra! Mommy loves you very much, but you have to take this medicine right now! Open your mouth, or Mommy will give you a spanking!"

"Nooo!" his mouth clamps down in a vise grip.

I swat his little behind, not hard, but just enough to send the message that I mean business.

"Whaaaahhhh!" The second those lips unlock, I dump the medicine down the hatch. He sputters a little and then gets madder than a wet hen when he realizes he's been medicated against his will.

I soften at the sound of him crying. I stroke his face and tell him that I love him and that I had to give him medicine for his own good.

"G'night, sugar pop. Momma loves you very, very much. I'll see you in the morning." In a way, I've won, but then why do I feel so bad? With a lump in my throat, I go back to bed and listen for the few minutes it takes for my son to fall asleep. Sometimes, with a toddler, all you can do is your best and hope tomorrow is an easier day.

How to Conduct a Romantic Interlude When a Two-Year-Old Lives at Your House

You and your man are the luckiest people in the world to be parents, but that doesn't mean you get lucky very often. With the sleep-challenged baby days a fading memory and a possible twinkle in your eyes for number two, here's your guide to, as writer Ken Gordon says, "dancing the bedroom-based Frug."

1. One day, as your twobie is finger painting on the deck, realize with a start that you haven't actually made mad, passionate love with your spouse lately.

2. Realize you haven't made love, period.

3. Wax nostalgic about the good-old days when the two of you put the "pair" in "Paradise by the Dashboard Lights."

4. Fret about the fact that the young scamp in your lives is rather prone to waking up at night and crawling into bed with Ma and Pa.

5. Decide to investigate your lingerie drawer for some nifty duds to wow your husband.

6. Attempt to pry open your lingerie drawer and realize it hasn't been opened in so long that clothes from other drawers are now jamming it.

7. Give up, knowing full well your husband would take you wearing a pillowcase at this point. In fact, the pillowcase thing is not a bad idea.

8. Cut the munchkin's nap by half an hour to ensure he won't be Mr. Livewire at 9:00 P.M.

9. Congratulate yourself on thinking this up.

10. Endure an insufferably cranky toddler the rest of the day.

11. Pop in a movie for the little grouch and steal away to the computer room to write a naughty e-mail to your husband at work.

12. With a surprised look on your face, greet your husband at the door and say, "Wow, you're home early."

13. Fill the hours between 4:00 P.M. and 9:00 P.M. with winks, wiggly eyebrow raises, double entendres (as if the kid would get a single entendre!), various incognito "love pats," and other flirty little build-ups.

14. Your husband, now grinning foolishly from ear to ear, readily agrees to bathe the youngster while you "get ready."

15. Brush, floss, apply eye cream (your usual routine). Get naked and wrap yourself in a Toronto Maple Leafs pillowcase your husband owns but has never actually used to cover a pillow. Figure the sports motif will only boost your cause.

16. At 9:30 fret about the fact that your toddler is somehow bouncing off the ceilings despite his shortened nap. Comprehend with dismay that he could now be what experts call "overtired."

17. At 9:45, after fifteen minutes of quiet from your two-year-old's room, your husband enters the "love shack" area of the home, still grinning.

18. Commence with the activity at hand, noting out of the corner of your eye the Leafs pillowcase now dangling from the candle sconce.

19. Just as the two of you are getting to the really good part, hear a squeak. The door is definitely opening, and your firstborn child is definitely entering the room.

20. Frantically dive under the covers like a pair of campers in a sudden rainstorm.

21. "Whatcha doin', Mommy?" your son asks, eyes wide with curiosity.

22. "Hey, buddy, you're supposed to be sleeping," your husband

manages to croak, peeking out from the covers. "Me and Mommy were just, you know, wrestling."

23. "Daddy, I skeered of mon-ters," the interloper declares, climbing up onto the bed covers.

24. Deep sigh. It's all over, you decide. Time to pack it in for the night and try to resume operations tomorrow.

25. Deposit the child at Grandma's for an hour the next evening, citing a vague excuse about "errands" you two have to run.

26. Have at it—and realize some things are worth waiting for.

Toy Story: Role-Playing, the Stuff of Life

Zoe, my feminine little niece, loves nothing more than to play with her minikitchen, her tea party set, or her doll accoutrements—strollers,

---

Doin' the Dough

For cheap and easy (and edible) play dough, mix the following ingredients together in a small pot:

> 1 cup flour
>
> 1 cup water
>
> 1 tablespoon oil
>
> 1 teaspoon salt
>
> 2 teaspoons cream of tartar
>
> drops of food coloring for color (as many as you like)

Stir continuously with a wooden spoon over medium heat until the dough begins to pull away from the side of the pot and form a dense ball. Allow the dough to cool about five to ten minutes, then knead it until it takes on a smooth texture. Store in a plastic bag. The dough will last for a few days depending on the humidity in your area.

highchairs, bathtubs, and so on. Toddlers at two-plus are keen observers of their surroundings and experiences and will mimic the scenarios and actions they witness from their thirty-six-inch perspectives. Since my brother and his wife became the parents of twin boys just before Zoe's second birthday, she's become Mom's grocery-shopping buddy. "She'll pretend she's opening the door of the minivan and then hop in for a 'ride,'" says Tina, my busy sister-in-law. "I'll ask her where she's going, and she says, 'grocery shopping.' Then she'll pretend to choose food items and put them away in her toy kitchen."

I talked about dolls in the previous chapter and how Zoe's imaginary play incorporates her life experience of two tiny babies in the house. You'd think she'd have her fill of babies, but Zoe loves to bathe her baby dolls, seat them in a dolly highchair, feed them, and wheel them around the house in her little stroller. It's a wonderful way for Zoe to make sense of the changes wrought by her new siblings, just as all imaginary play helps toddlers come to grips with the doings of their universe.

No matter how PC you are, your toddler will probably play in a gender-stereotyped way—at least some of the time. Ezra will cart around his cousin's dolls for a few minutes, but most often he quickly gives up on the girl stuff and looks for ways to turn Zoe's toys into weapons. Meanwhile, Zoe might scoop up some sand with Ez's dump truck and then ditch that activity for more doll time. But many toys appeal to both girls and boys at this age. Here are just a few:

- *Plush hand puppets* for cuddles and drama feed into a tot's wide-eyed wonder world.
- *Easy-to-open, round-ended scissors* for shredding magazines, water-based glue, and stickers make for the incredibly rewarding—and messy—activity of putting together a first scrapbook.
- *Balls* for kicking around boost large-motor skills and physical activity.

Fabulous Freebie: Roll It, Pat It, Mark It with a C. Is there anything more fabulous than mushing a lump of squishy Play-Doh in your fingers?

Add a mini rolling pin, plastic cookie cutters, and kid-friendly knives, and you've got a world of toddler fun at your fingertips. You can show your little playmate how to roll a piece of dough to make a snake, and then make hissing noises for kicks. Some toddlers simply like to squeeze the yummy-feeling dough through their fingers, while others get in touch with their inner Rodin and get quite artsy fartsy about their squishable sculptures. If you'd like, you can form letters of the alphabet with dough and reinforce the ABCs while you play. Making play dough (see previous sidebar for a recipe) is also a great project to do with your toddler. Allow him to add food coloring or knead the cooling dough.

Pandemonium in Public, Polite Patrons, and Papa in Palm Beach

Feeling a little droopy? That might be because your two-and-a-half-year-old is running circles around you—literally. Many moms report unexpected weight loss when mothering toddlers. It's because they are on the chase every waking hour.

Another energy stealer: the public tantrum. You know it, girlfriend: Nothing robs you of confidence and deflates your mood more than when your carefully reared child decides to have a conniption in front of the watching world. In Toddler Tutorial 6, get the lowdown on public tantrums, how to avert them, cope with them, and blow them off when they are over. Of course, with my tempestuous tot, I have loads of stories detailing his blowing a gasket while out and about with his ma. One of those sagas is revealed here in "Life with Ez." Amazing, isn't it, how even though our little stinkers can be so stinky, their extended family still wants to spend quality time with them? When you need a break—especially after downsizing a supersized blowout at McDonald's—it's great to tap family members so they can share the joy. Read about keeping close ties to long-distance loved ones in here as well. And perk up, because toddler tantrum time is almost over!

Milemarker: Energizer Bunnies, Every One

Wheeee! Two-and-a-half-year-olds have energy to burn, and they need lots of physical activity to help them burn it off. Climbing the monkey bars, pedaling a tricycle, kicking a ball, and running from Monster Mommy (and giggling his little head off) are all ways for Mr. Verve-and-Nerve to run off steam, build a good body image, and master his large-motor skills. Experts say there is another bonus to physical action at this age: "The connections built between neurons in the brain, known as neural pathways, are formulated by persistent physical as well as cognitive activity."[1] So take a walk, chase your toddler, stay close as he attempts to climb playground apparatus, kick a ball in the backyard—it's all good for the boy (and his mommy)!

Life with Ez: Public Tantrum Edition

The other day I took Ezra to the doctor to have his ears checked. Of course Jonah tagged along; he immediately claimed that his ears were "plugged" too and that he needed a "checkup." Being as it was the height of cold and flu season, the waiting room was teeming with customers in various states of croup, rhinitus, and strep. Parents and their malaise-ridden offspring huddled in dismal little clumps, peering warily at other clumps and the germs they seemed to radiate. Green snot was the order of the day, and no one was being overly friendly.

For once my two yo-yos were pretty much the most robust of the bunch, Ez's problem being only a suspected ear infection (though it turned out that he had one of those fun double ear infections). So Jonah and Ez ran around the room, grabbing toys and munching on carrots. Yeah, carrots. For some reason, right before we left for the doc's, Jonah thought it would be a grand idea to grab a couple of bags of those mini-carrots for a snack. I figured, *Hey, it's about a hundred times more healthy than his run-of-the-mill snack ideas (candy and anything Gummified), so why not?*

The carrots, for whatever reason, hit Ez all wrong, and he puked orange particles all over himself, his parka, his boots, the doctor's toys, and the floor. And then he started shrieking. It was the public meltdown, every mother's nightmare.

You could almost hear the collective gasp of horror from the moms in each clump. Was it my imagination, or were the other mothers glaring at me? Man! It wasn't as if I'd made the kid heave carrots all over the place!

Well, I ordered myself to remain quite calm and mop up the mess in short order, all the while comforting my banshee child. And then, in the midst of it all, my girlfriend's impossibly chic, together, wonderful, and perfect sister breezed through the front door, impossibly chic child in tow. Now this little Technicolor drama of sight and sound (and smell, too) was being played out not just in front of strangers, but in front of someone I knew, a Mother-of-the-Year type to boot. She pretended not to know me, which was just as well. It took all my gumption to calm my freaked-out child, to bring down the decibel level of his screams from piercing to just plain loud.

Silently I flogged myself for giving him carrots when I knew he wasn't at all used to them. Gummi worms? Those he would have kept down his gullet, no doubt. And now I had a bellowing two-year-old on my hands, twenty hairy eyeballs looking my way, and the pleasant aroma of regurgitation wafting around my miserable clump.

I know what it means to feel the pain.

All the World's a Stage for Toddler Tantrums

Whether in a doctor's office, grocery store, restaurant, or airplane (oh my), nothing strikes fear into the heart of a parent like her toddler's public tantrums. Why? Because no matter how many times you've told yourself that everyone's kids have them, somehow you still manage to feel like a loser when it's *your* precious baby brat raising Cain in the cereal aisle.

Tantrums touch on our deepest insecurities as moms and dads. What kind of child have we produced? We believe that our kid's behavior reflects on her parents' ability (or lack thereof) to keep everything under control. Many people out there in the world are sympathetic, but the truth is, some do make snap judgments about you when your child is bellowing. Without knowing the specifics of your situation—no nap, late lunch, an oncoming cold—they can zing you with these laser glares that say "You are inept" in fifty languages.

Blow these people off because, clearly, their brains are starved for oxygen. Do they have a better plan than yours (which we'll get to momentar-

---

✎ Voices: Because Misery Loves Company

Here are a couple of public meltdown stories for your reading diversion. The first one is pretty basic, standard tantrum material, but the second one actually has a happy ending. Here goes:

"Our little family went to Florida to visit my grandparents just before our firstborn was two. My husband, a huge baseball fan, took us to see a spring training game. We thought, *What fun for our little guy to learn about Daddy's favorite sport!* Well, he didn't sit still for most of the game, so we walked around the concourse of the ballpark. A speed throw was set up on the concourse for fans, and maybe a future big leaguer, to test how fast they could throw a ball at a canvas backdrop and have the speed of the throw displayed for bragging rights. Sheldon, not able to really throw a ball, was allowed by the man working the booth to just toss the balls a bit and be oh-so-cute.

"After a few tries, the patience of the people in line wore thin, and we told Sheldon it was time to go so the other people waiting

ily)? Nope, I didn't think so! But whether a blowout happens at Starbucks or the library or your family room, certain truths remain: A toddler tizzy is not an indication of inadequate parenting. It's just a two-year-old displaying incontrovertible evidence of his normal development!

What he needs during those messy little episodes is some grown-up direction from you to get you both to the other side (where both you and he can breathe again). Receiving that direction teaches tots that they can learn to cope with stormy emotions. As your toddler grows, you can provide the input he needs to calm himself and to set some personal limits.

Communal tantrums—where the populace and their dogs are all privy to every scream and snort—are becoming a bigger issue nowadays,

could have their turn. He did not want to go. We indulged him a minute or so more, then picked him up—he wasn't about to walk away of his own free will—and turned to leave. He threw himself backward hard enough that we almost dropped him, so we put him down to hold hands and walk. He did not like that any better and promptly threw himself facedown on the concourse pavement and, screaming, proceeded to bang and kick his little hands and feet on the ground—you know, the way kids do in cartoons. My husband and I stood there in amazement because Sheldon has never thrown a fit like this before. Immediately, ballpark security and staff rushed over, wanting to know if he'd been hurt or had fallen down. We just calmly stood there, watching him carry on, and said, 'No, he's having a fit because he's not getting his way. We're just waiting for him to calm down so we can go back to our seats.' After a bit we told Sheldon he was not going to get his way. People were staring— shouldn't he think about getting up off the ground? He just turned

(continued)

especially for dual-income families. When Mom and Dad both work, they want to spend most of their nonworking hours with the kiddies. This means many parents are taking toddlers into adult situations such as restaurants, adult get-togethers, and even movie theaters.

The more you go out, the greater the chances of your toddler having a public meltdown. All the world's a stage, right? And when Miss Diva pulls out all the stops and smoke is coming out of her ears, people want to pull up a chair and see what's gonna happen next. This means you, as Mother, will be dragged to the front and center of this little drama, and really, the peanut—or popcorn, as it were—gallery is just itching to see you perform. *What's Mom going to do now?* It's easy to become very anxious at this point. Burning cheeks, tense muscles, not making eye contact

his head, saw that we were serious, and got up. We picked him up, dusted him off, and went back to watch the game, shaking our heads and chuckling. He never threw another fit like that again."

—Linda

"One classic tantrum story took place in a grocery store in the middle of January. My oldest, Gabe, was four and a half, Maggie was just three, Eva was a fifteen-month-old toddler, and I was obviously pregnant with Malachi. We had been out for errands all morning, and I thought we could swing one more stop. We desperately needed milk, but with three little ones bundled in winter parkas, I was wishing, not for the first time, that the grocery store had a drive-through window!

"Gabe was asking for candy, which should be outlawed in grocery stores! When I said no to the candy, my usually controlled eldest starting crying. I paid for the milk and, hefting Eva and the milk, told Gabe and Maggie to follow me to the van. Well, Gabe

with anyone—I've been there. But when your child's tantrum sparks your emotions to the point where you are about to lose it too, you must take a deep breath and try to calm down. If you also have a meltdown, I'll tell ya: People will start selling tickets.

Why can't toddlers pick more appropriate places for going ballistic? Like behind closed doors for example? It's because public places, such as stores and malls and libraries, are very exciting and stimulating for little ones. Plus, Mommy and Daddy say no in such places with alarming regularity. No to the rubberized frog thing. No to the raspberry-filled donut. No to the huge, glossy—and expensive-to-replace—library book. Frustration mounts quickly, and any number of triggers are like matches to a gas can. *Ka-BOOM!*

dropped to the floor and started screaming! I told Maggie to hold Eva's hand as I tried to pick up Gabe, and Eva started crying because she didn't want to hold Maggie's hand! So now I had two kids throwing a tantrum, and it kept getting worse.

"Gabe started stiffening in that 'make your body as large and cumbersome as possible and grab everything in sight' move, which made it almost impossible to carry him. We 'gracefully' stumbled to the van, my face burning with embarrassment, and I loaded my screaming children into the van. Just then an older woman came up to me, and I thought for sure she was from social services! She said the most unexpected, wonderful thing: 'Dear, don't you worry. Mine was the same way, and now he's a grown man—and a fine one at that. Your boy will turn out just fine.'

"I know that lady was an angel and that God was watching over me and caring for me, even in the midst of my double tantrum disaster."

—Amy

Toddler Tutorial 6:
How to Deal with a Kid
Having Open-Air Histrionics

1. Block out the World

As best you can, turn your efforts into a laser beam that homes in on your child and how you're going to calm her down. Don't let other people's stares make you more anxious. My friend Ann remembers her little girl's insistence on blowing up at the department store: "When Abby was two and three, she would routinely throw fits in Meijer's. When she did that I would take her to the men's underwear aisle and wait it out. It usually took about five minutes of her crying and screaming and my standing there looking at her. Nobody hangs out in the men's underwear aisle anyway, and if they do, they shouldn't."

2. Breathe

Take big gulps of calming air to settle your nerves. Hey, it works!

3. Help Your Child Regain Control

Hold her or stand nearby and say reassuring things like, "You're okay. It's time to calm down."

4. Keep Your Funny Bone Activated

Perhaps one day you'll laugh at the time Cassie practically coughed up a lung she was crying so hard at the bowling alley, because you wouldn't let her run into the next lane. (Not today, but someday, surely.) When her daughter Libby flopped to her belly and wailed loudly at some indignity in the bookstore, Monica tried in vain to soothe her daughter. An older man peered around the bookshelf at the ruckus, and Monica's heart sank. "I was prepared for a lecture or a dirty look," she said. "But the guy just smiled and said, 'Two?' 'How'd you know,' I asked, rhetorically. 'I just knew,' he said."

5. Lay the Good Stuff on Thick

It helps to pour on the praise when your child is a little angel on an outing. Say, "I had such a wonderful time shopping with you today. Wasn't that fun?" She'll be proud of herself, and next time maybe she'll remember it pays to be good.

Happy Meals

"We've seen a big increase in parents' eating out with their children," says Michael Mount, spokesperson for the National Restaurant Association in Washington, D.C. "Both parents are working, and they want to be with their kids instead of having to spend time cooking dinner."[2] If your family is anything like ours, you will probably spend much more time in a restaurant with small children than our parents ever did, even if you're a full-time mother. We go out quite often, not just because I don't much like cooking, but because I write a semiregular column for *The Grand Rapids Press* called "Dining Out with Kids." I touched on this topic in my last book, *O for a Thousand Nights to Sleep,* so I won't go into great detail. But as you know, it's a whole new can of worms dining out with a toddler.

My Twenty-Eight-Month-Old

"Judah is my tester. He will test me on everything, especially when it comes to the fridge. He knows he's not supposed to get into the fridge by himself, but he will go and open it, and I'll find him in a corner somewhere, dumping Parmesan cheese from the canister into his mouth!"
                                                              —Margaret

Here are a few tips for keeping pint-sized patrons happy enough so everyone can finish their meal in peace:

- *Discuss the rules* (no yelling or throwing food) ahead of time and review them in the car on the way over.

- *Keep kids busy* with books, crayons, and nonmessy, quiet toys.
- *Bring light snacks* (saltines, Goldfish) to ease the wait for the real food to arrive.
- *Include your little one in the conversation.* It's hard not to eagerly fill your mate in on the highs and lows of the day, but try to look at the evening from your toddler's point of view. If she just sits there, she's going to feel restless and left out. But if she feels she's one of the gang, she's going to be much more agreeable all the way around.
- *If your child misbehaves, take him outside and have a short but penetrating chat about his behavior.* (Notify the waitress you are doing this or she'll freak and think you've stiffed her on the bill.) Tell your wild-and-woolly kid that he'd better stop shrieking or jumping on the seat or whatever—or no ice cream.
- *Remember, he wants to be at the table with Mommy and Daddy, but it is excruciatingly hard to sit still.* Case in point: Hoping for a relaxing night out as a family, Leanne took her two-year-old son Braden out for dinner. So much for serenity. "He wanted to jump in the booth, turn around and touch the people behind us, climb over the seat, and go outside and play," Leanne remembers with a grimace. "I thought, *Why can't he just sit still for one simple meal, even for half an hour?*" Of course Braden was thinking that he had already been trapped in a car seat for fifteen minutes and that it sure was interesting and exciting at this restaurant. And how about that cool squishy feeling when he jumps up and down on the seat of his booth? Keep in mind that a leisurely dinner out is pretty much a fantasy. If you want that, get a baby-sitter. Expect reasonable behavior for half an hour—if you have lots of distractions to keep your toddler occupied. A few ideas for when the crayons get old: Make towers out of creamers and jam packets, stack crayons like Jenga pieces, or play "hockey" with spoons and a creamer. And don't forget to tip your server well!

Over the Hill to Grandma's House (or "Grandma's Not over the Hill–She's in Palm Beach!")

In our mobile age, Grandma is unlikely to live over the hill anymore. She may be an hour by car or even a transcontinental flight away from her favorite two-year-old. Even during their toddler years, children are enriched by contact with extended family, including geographically distant ones. But how do we keep the bonds of family strong across the miles? It's not as hard as you think. Even young toddlers can "talk" on the phone or look at pictures of Granny in Sacramento and Opa in Vancouver. To help her eighteen-month-old daughter recognize family members, Christa

Slimming Moves for Moms

Still feeling a little less than svelte even though it's been a couple of years (but who's counting?) since you delivered the turbo tot? You're not alone. Many moms struggle with their weight many moons after they thought they would have their old bods back. Experts say weight loss is really a simple matter of eating less and moving more. Well, duh! But when you think about it, that's what works. One of the best notions I've heard on the subject comes from newswoman Deborah Norville. Her tip for keeping shipshape, even in the midst of a busy career and family life? Vigorous playtimes! When Norville couldn't squeeze in a workout after work—and who among us can blame her for that?—she would chase her young sons around the house a few times. This way, Norville reported, she could be a fun mommy and burn some extra calories at the same time. So kick a ball around the backyard, play tag, or grab some floor hockey sticks for a scrimmage on the deck. It's a great way to get your heart rate up and get closer to your child at the same time—brilliant! So move it, girl!

made a picture book with photographs of different relatives on each page. It reads, "Grace, Grace, who do you see? I see Uncle Ryan (or Papa, Nana, whoever) looking at me." Christy says Grace loves to look at the pictures, and she seems to recognize the faces of her long-lost loved ones when they come to visit.

The key in helping your toddler forge a strong bond with his long-distance relatives is to talk about them all the time. It's comforting to know that people other than Mom and Dad care about him, so assure him often of Grandma and Grandpa's love.

Invent creative ways of making your parents and in-laws a vital part of your everyday life. Fax Junior's latest "drawing" to Grandpa at his work—he'll post it with pride. E-mail the proud grandparents with the very latest developments in their grandchild's life. Send photos as often as you can. Ask your father-in-law to send postcards from Boca and chat with your toddler about the picture on the front. "Ooooh—you've got a letter from Granddad! He must love you so much, Ethan. Look at that funny doggie on the picture!" Your enthusiasm is catchy, especially at this tender age. Homemade audiotapes of the grandparents or other special relatives reading bedtime stories are a wonderful way for your child to hear those beloved voices on a regular basis. With Webcams and whatnot, the two parties can even see each other as they chat (or as Grandma chats and your toddler nods at the phone.)

Food also links us to people, and there are fun ways to incorporate favorite family dishes in the process of strengthening ties. Compile a family recipe book—maybe a scrapbook with recipes and photos of the cook—and announce to your little one whose recipe you've made: "Grandma Sally loves making these cookies. When I was little, I used to help her stir just like you did today."

We were visiting my parents in Winnipeg for Christmas when my mom served pierogies (Polish/Ukrainian dumplings) and fleisch perishke (Mennonite meat buns). Jonah complained he didn't like the pierogies, which was akin to saying he wished he were Italian/Swedish/Mexican and not Polish/Ukrainian/Mennonite. He got quite the lecture on feeling pride in one's ethnic background and how no Polish/Ukrainian/Menno kid worth his salt would turn down some lip-smacking cheese pierogies. (Hey, it wasn't like we made the kid eat the prune kind.) Wilted, Jonah ate his food without further comment and (I knew this was coming) asked for seconds. Ezra just ate whatever was set before him. I think he would have scarfed down some of my dad's famously repulsive headcheese (another "delicacy" of the Mennonites) if his Opa had dared to offer it. But my point—and I do have one—is that it's never too early to introduce your toddler to the foods and folkways of his family heritage. In fact, the earlier you launch these ethnic culinary campaigns, the better. Maybe your parents would be interested in sending care packages of favorite family foods? Hey, it never hurts to ask!

Faith Builder

"Be careful, little eyes, what you see, be careful, little eyes, what you see. For the Father up above is looking down in love, so be careful, little eyes, what you see." This song is one of the great Sunday-school classics, and it's a tuneful little ditty that packs a wallop of theological truth. My friend Ann has a tradition of singing this song to her toddlers when they are being changed. (Bath time is another good window of opportunity for this.) For each "category" following "Be careful" ("little eyes," "little ears," etc.), Ann talks about a good thing to see or hear and a bad thing to see or hear or for little hands to do. "Hattie, a good thing to hear is people singing about God, and a bad thing to hear is people fighting and calling each other names." This little game is a touchstone for talking about the way we're molded by what we see, hear, and do.

A note about family visits: Making family visits a priority sends the message that you care about being close and connected. Whether Grandma and Grandpa bunk at your place—and that's another story—or at the Best Western, try to make sure your toddler gets lots of one-on-one time with them. Grab your spouse and go out on a date—remember those?—and let your little one bond with the patriarch and matriarch for a while. If you're hovering around all the time, the kid will never get to know his grandparents. If you make an effort to build a relationship now, while your munchkin is still a toddler, you'll be amazed at the closeness he shares with his kin someday.

Toy Story: From Barney to Beethoven

We have a Barney banjo at our house that is incredibly popular with just about any child between the ages of one and five who rummages through our toy box. You strum the banjo, and it plays some sort of kiddie ditty. (We've had that thing for four years now, and despite our efforts to hide it or our hopes that the batteries will run dead, the banjo continues to appear, much like a crop circle, in our toy box. The batteries will never, ever go dead, we've decided, because they have not in four years, so why would they now?) Despite the fact that we also have all manner of mini-guitars in our toy box, and real instruments like harmonicas and bongos, that yippee-skippee purple thing is just the bomb, especially with two-year-olds. Why? Because little flat pickers love making things happen. That passion combined with their fondness for music—well, the Barney banjo is as good as it gets. Any musical toy is excellent for toddlers, especially those that feature annoying, repetitive features such as flashing lights and loud, obnoxious music sung out of key by Elmo or Barney or whoever. Because the kids love these furry little monsters and sappy purple dinosaurs already—even if they drive parents around the bend—making music with them is delightful and rewarding. Grin and bear it. Today Barney, tomorrow Beethoven? Hey, it could happen.

Other much less noisy toys for two-and-a-half-year-olds:

- *Puzzles.*
- *Construction toys* that snap together, like Lego or Duplo blocks. These are loads of fun for toddlers with their new and improved coordination and hand strength.
- *Durable plastic kiddie tape recorders* for little Mr. Independence to play his own music tapes. (You might want to show him how to put the tape into the player the first few times, although he will probably try to do it himself.)

Fabulous Freebie: When Jonah was two, he turned an open box lying on its side into a bakery oven and an unopened package of pantyhose into a cake. "What're you doing, sweets?" I asked him, observing his intense concentration as he slid the hose into the box, closed the flaps, and then peered inside the cracks. "Makin' a cake, Mommy," he said, as if, my goodness, I should have known that. Baby Whisperer Tracy Hogg reminded me of that sweet memory: "Toddlers…are filled with wonder," she writes. "They're little scientists in the making. Their eyes and minds are wide open and ready to explore. They don't need an object to stimulate them. At birthdays and holidays, why do you think toddlers often go for the boxes and not the objects inside? It's because the box can become anything the child would like, while most new toys have to be 'operated' in a certain way. Cartons provide hours of imaginative entertainment. Children can hide in them, use them to play house or fort. They can jump on them, crush them, and there's no right or wrong way to play with them either."[3]

Two Kids, Toilet Teaching (Part 1), and the Tremendous TP Tube

So, were you wondering when I would ever get around to potty training? I'm sure many of you were, and here's the reason I held off until now: I'm an advocate of later training as opposed to pushing a toddler too early. I hate messes, and for me, waiting until my son was good and ready just made sense. Whatever philosophy you happen to hold on the topic, here's my little guide to toilet teaching, which is slightly more complicated than Dave Barry's (see the next chapter). But before we wander into the world of potty, first you'll gain some hints for easing the transition from one child to two. It's not easy, but it's also not as brain intensive as many claim it to be. I myself was sorely worried about how I would handle a newborn and a tyke, but somehow I muddled through, and you can too! (Actually, two can be great once you get the hang of it.) Finally, I cap off chapter 10 with a glowing tribute to the toilet-paper tube. (Fitting, don't you think, here in the middle of discussing all things commode-ious—and odious?) Hey, if your kid's not quite using toilet paper correctly yet, he may as well have some fun with the tube!

Milemarker: "Me Do! No, You Do!"

Two-year-olds are total yo-yos. Your cutie's job is to convince you she can handle anything. Your job is to convince her you need to stand by. Toddlers whirl off on their own one minute and the next come rushing back to your arms. Experts say there's a sudden shift in parenting a child this age. Nurturing and responding to your little one is still a big chunk of the job, but now you must also—within reason—hand over some of the control. Offer options on the little things, and she probably won't push too hard on the biggies. Toddlers love the power of choice: "Tonight, do you want the story about the bunny or the story about the spider? Would you like grape juice or apple juice?" This helps them feel as if they have some say in their lives and lets them practice making decisions, a key element of the can-do kid.

The Two-Kid Drill

"Wednesday night was loads of fun," mom Charlotte told me. "While Brian was playing paintball with the youth group at church, the toilet backed up and overflowed while Anna was brushing her teeth. Baby Noah, mind you, was also in the bathroom, lying on the bathmat. I hauled Noah downstairs and put him in his baby swing, stuck a movie in for Anna, and raced back upstairs to contain the pee water spreading all over the bathroom floor. After I got the bathroom back in order, I came down and sank into the couch, wearily planning to watch *Beauty and the Beast* for two seconds before putting Noah to bed. Suddenly Anna cried, 'Mom! Look!'

"Noah had thrown up all over his clean footie pajamas, the ones I had put on him right before saving him (and them) from the toilet-water tidal wave. Of course, while I had been upstairs, Anna had given Noah her beloved blankie, the one she cannot sleep without, the one that was now covered with baby puke! This was *less than ten minutes* after the toilet overflowed, mind you. When Brian came home, an hour after the kids' bedtime, the blankie was still drying, and Anna and I were watching the ten o'clock news. We were up that night with Noah, too, who had some stomach virus. I told Brian he'd picked a really good night not to be home!"

As Charlotte's story so eloquently illustrates, having more than one child means double the chances for something to go awry. As you know, little kids are wild cards when it comes to random domestic disasters, and babies are even less predictable. Finessing the two-kid drill can take lots of, well, finesse.

So how do you cope when you're short on sleep and long on laundry? Clearly, there is a huge change in logistics when Numero Dos shows up.

Time for a Big-Boy Bed?

Some people can't wait to switch their toddler from the crib to the thrilling new big-boy or big-girl bed. I have always resisted this with every fiber of my being because I am way too sappy, and it kills me to see this huge symbol of babyhood being packed away. But since the kid probably shouldn't be sleeping in a crib when he's about to enter kindergarten, you may want to consider making the big move. Really, anytime between two and three is fine to transition unless your cutie would be in danger of falling out of the bed. (Even my friend Nancy, with her beautiful and tall future-supermodel child, Eva, didn't switch until her toddler was almost three.)

Weeks before the Big Switch, talk up the concept of a bed. Invite your budding bed-sleeper to pick out some sheets and a comforter, or maybe a new stuffed animal to sleep with in the new digs. If even the thrilling new Clifford the Big Red Dog comforter and glow-in-the-dark Bob the Tomato aren't enough to win your scamp over to the bed, guide him in saying a long, satisfying good-bye to the crib. Jonah had to run back a few nights to his closet and say "Buh-bye" to his old friend.

Suddenly you have two human beings who need your attention and nurturing, and that can get complicated.

Here are some nuts-and-bolts ideas for smoothing out the crimp a twofer puts in your domestic life:

- *Playtime.* "Wear" your baby and play with your child. Wearing your infant in a sling or backpack is a great way to free your hands for toddler time. Play Candyland with your big girl while her baby brother snoozes in your baby carrier. Help your toddler with potty time as the baby watches the world from your sling. You get the picture. Numero Uno won't feel as resentful of the new bambino if

Voices: Tips from the Toddler Trenches

"My two eldest were only twenty-two months apart. As much as they may argue, Caitlin and Meg are very close. I think the key was keeping Caitlin involved in caring for Meg so she knew that she wasn't being replaced. There's never been a jealousy problem between them. We really strive to teach our kids to reach out and help with the littler ones. They feel important, they become close to their siblings, and they learn that they aren't the center of the universe. They're important, and they have something to give to others."

—Traci

"Buy a double stroller and go for lots of walks. When I had Abigail, Naomi was only nineteen months and Reuben was three and a half. That was a hard time. I somehow got them all on the same afternoon sleep schedule. That really helped me because I needed the nap too. I would also suggest signing [using sign language] with your baby and toddler. This gives you nice quiet communication. I have been doing this with Chloe [her fourth child], and I have enjoyed watching my other kids learn the signs too. They get excited because you don't constantly have to be saying, "Hold on a minute while I put the baby down."

- *Your toddler, the entertainer.* He can be a help to you—and thus to the whole family—just by doing what kids do best: entertaining their little siblings. It's amazing, really, how attached an infant and an older sibling can become. If you ever do feel that inevitable sense of guilt that you're neglecting your firstborn, remember that you've just given her the best present she could ever want or need—a sibling. Nothing will warm the cockles of your heart more than seeing your two children exhibit signs of love for each

they know what she is saying and can communicate with her on some level. Also, when Abigail, the youngest, was a newborn, I worried about putting her in the bassinet because I was afraid that one of the other two would tip it over when they were trying to get a glimpse of her. I folded the bassinet's legs underneath it and put the whole thing inside the portacrib so there was no way they could dump the baby. It worked great, and I did not feel like I had to be watching every minute."

—Dawn

"When Mark and I arrived home from the hospital with Morgan, Elle took one half-loving look at her and then proceeded to lie down on the kitchen floor and kick and scream! At that moment I knew that I was in for some challenges. From the beginning it has been important for Elle and me to have one-on-one time, whether it meant playing a game while Morgan was sleeping or taking a trip to the park when Daddy could be with Morgan. Having these little 'traditions' with Elle helped us stay connected. We experienced the

(continued)

other (in between periods of exhibiting less positive emotions, of course). I won't lie to you: Life is going to get busier, noisier, more cluttered, and less restful, especially for the first few months. But, honestly, the work won't double or triple with two kids like some helpful yahoos have probably told you it would. It's really more like one and a half times more work, which you won't even really notice because of that whole sleep deprivation thing. (Hey, if I can do it, so can you!)

- *An extra set of arms.* Your older toddler can pick up diapers and washcloths and even hand you the remote when you're nursing.

same thing when Anna was born. Morgan was twenty-eight months by then, and that whole first summer she refused to wear anything but a bike helmet and a bathing suit. It was her way of rebelling against the baby, I guess. We spent lots of one-on-one time with her, too, and gradually she started wearing other clothes!"

—Deone

"Having five little ones under the age of eight, I *highly* recommend 'special time with Daddy'! This seems to be a somewhat natural process. As my lap got smaller, somehow Daddy's felt more comfortable, especially with my boys, Gabe and Malachi. When the next baby was born, they would see that Mommy was busy and figure they best not let go of Daddy or he may get busy too! Malachi likes to say to Steve, 'Snuggle with Daddy time?' And then Steve picks Malachi up, cuddles with him, and gives him the one-on-one attention he needs. It usually doesn't take too long to fill his 'touch tank.' Another thing I have done is fill up a special basket with new or special toys/games/puzzles that the older kids can do independently. I take it down for short periods of time when I know I will be busy

She'll get a boost in confidence, too, especially if you praise her for being such a big help.

- *Bathing*. Obviously, until the baby is six months old and can sit safely in a bath seat, you can't really dunk 'em at the same time (which later will become a marvelous time-saver). What can you do with Zaza while you give Lulu a bath? You could always employ the time-honored solution of setting Baby in a bouncy seat while you bathe the big sister (or take a shower yourself). Some moms successfully have their toddler "help" bathe the baby, though I must admit my Jonah wasn't too excited about that job.

with the baby. This helps them feel like they have something special too. I live by the supply-and-demand theory: If Mommy is in demand, *everyone* wants her, so supply a substitute!"

—Amy

"This, too, shall pass. It's definitely rough going in the beginning, especially if your toddler feels jealous. So be sure to make time for the toddler, giving her extra affection, alone time, and a little leeway in regard to any bad behavior that surfaces (they may regress a bit). Using a breast pump full time for nursing also worked great for me. I started that when Ellie was about four months. She was a forty-five-minute 'snacker,' and while La Leche may have had advice that would have helped me change her habits, I wasn't up to researching it and trying to make it work. I had Avery demanding my attention during those long nursing sessions, and I couldn't expect her to wait for me for such long periods. Instead, I pumped for ten to fifteen minutes every three to four hours. Sounds like a lot of work, but it actually worked *much* better for me, and I felt freed up."

—Jane

Perhaps, if your child is a doll fan, you could have her swab the doll while you hose off the baby. Collecting supplies is always key when bathing a little one, but add a toddler to the mix and it becomes even more important to the success of the operation. Keeping towels, soaps, and shampoos (and toys for the big kid) in an easy-access bucket or cupboard will make for a smoother bath time.

Quotable

"Toddlerhood clearly marks the end of infancy. It's also a sneak preview of adolescence. In fact, many experts think of this period in the same vein as the teenage years, because a similar separation process is underway."   —Tracy Hogg

- *Bedtime.* When it's time for bed, who will give your older child the time and attention he's used to as part of his nighttime routine? It's time to divide and conquer. If your partner is around at night, split bedtime duties, with one of you feeding and rocking the baby and one of you cuddling and reading *The Very Hungry Caterpillar* to your toddler. Switch off if you want to get in on both kids' slumber rituals. Or you could put the baby to bed first (or second, depending on what time he eats his last meal of the day) and then spend cozy time with your two-year-old. Sometimes, though, he's going to have to come to grips with the fact that life has changed since the baby came. Mommy may not have time to read his favorite book three times and sing every stanza of "Alice's Camel" every single night. And you know what? He'll live. He'll even grow as a little person as he comes to understand that he is not the center of the universe anymore. As long as you're not shortchanging him every single night of the week to care for Baby, your firstborn should be okay. Letting someone else's needs come before your own? Not a bad lesson to learn, even if you are two.

Taking the "Toil" Out of the "Toilet" (Toilet Teaching, Part 1)

Let me say right up front that I have never actually potty trained a toddler. My son Jonah was three years and three months before he was trained completely. But I know most people attempt to "toilet teach" their children between ages two and three (apparently "potty training" is now a passé term, though I may slip back and forth between the archaic terminology and the new, socially acceptable phrase). Possibly the best tip I have heard on this subject was from a former coworker of mine. "I waited until all my kids were three," she said, "and then they were potty trained in a week."

That little morsel of wisdom stuck with me probably because I also heard horror stories of people trying to train their tots earlier and then having to scrape poop off of furniture and appliances. Cautionary tales of public accidents frightened me into waiting until my toddler was technically a preschooler. Who wants to cope with the ordeal of having your lap soaked in pee while sitting at a hockey game and having no jacket to cover yourself? Not me! Truly, I'd rather change diapers till the cows come home (where are those cows everyone always talks about anyway?) than mop up the diaspora of someone's bowel extrusions. At least in a diaper, the mess is contained—usually.

This was my line of reasoning in waiting until Jonah seemed utterly and completely ready to manage his own business end. Yes, we endured many a comment from the preceding generation, which only privately bothered me and only after he had actually turned three. The best part, though, was that my coworker was right: When Jonah started training, that was that. Within a week he was trained, and within a month or two he was dry through the night with hardly any messes at all (she said smugly). Of course, he was three, so how smug can I really be?

Though he was officially high and dry at three, we did start planting clues in his tender two-year-old mind about his "underweared" future. We indoctrinated him gently, using some soft-sell propaganda like the "Bear and the Big Blue House" potty video, which I highly recommend. We also read books with plot lines that involve toilets, body parts, human waste, and so on. These books always jubilantly hailed Training Day as a day above all days and ended happily with the toddler in question gleefully making use of his new elimination skills, his euphoric parents beaming nearby. I would also, with elaborate casualness, ask him periodically if he was interested in the potty. "Nope," he would say, equally offhand.

Well then, we sure weren't about to push it, because parents who push their children into potty training… Well, bad things happen to those people! (Don't they?) Of course I come from a family of advanced potty trainers. I myself was trained at fourteen months, apparently. And my father? According to family lore, he was trained at ten months. *Ten months!* Of course, each time this story is told I discover he was trained a little earlier. I'm sure by the time all my children and nephews and nieces are using the commode of their own volition they will hear about Opa being dry prenatally and not requiring diapers to begin with. All that to say, I didn't want to push, per se, but there was still a little voice inside that said, "Push, you slacker you! Do ya want the kid to be wearing Huggies at the prom?"

I'm sure many of you have experienced this inner turmoil of wondering how pushy is too pushy and how laid-back is too laid-back. It's enough to send you to the spa for a facial. Or at least to that box of Oreos you've got stashed in your lingerie drawer.

Is toilet training really rocket science, or is it as easy as your sister-in-law said it was with her eight perfect children *(grrrr)*? I've only managed to impart the secrets of lavatory finesse to one child, and as I've said, he was technically a preschooler.

In the eventuality that you would like to train or "teach" your little one how to use the bathroom before he's three—or before Aunt Mildred has a coronary over it—I've rounded up some tips to light the way.

- *The scoop on potty readiness is really all about this:* Are the muscles of your toddler's anus and bladder ready for action? She might grow up to be a Rhodes Scholar, but those special little muscles of hers have a mind of their own. If they ain't ready, she ain't ready. (Take that, Aunt Mildred.) Usually these muscles are developed between eighteen and thirty-six months, so experts say hold off until your tot is two for optimum success. Since there's not really a surefire way of knowing what's doin' down there, here are a few more signals to watch for: Does she seem interested in watching members of the family use the toilet? Is she aware of the urge to go, even when wearing a diaper, and does she tell you? Is she beginning to remove her pants without your help? All these things make it easier for her to be successful when the time comes.
- *Feed your child high-fiber foods and lots of water so he will be highly motivated to unload often.*
- *People hold differing opinions as to what the next step should be:* Do we buy a potty or one of those ringlike miniseats that prevent a

True Colors

When your toddler's between two and three, she'll pick up a fun new skill: being able to tell you the minivan is green, her favorite sweater is "lellow," and the Gummi octopus she wants is pink and purple. You can boost your tyke's true colors by labeling them when you speak ("Yes, that's a green worm!"), instituting color-theme days (on "Purple Day," for example, drink grape juice, have her wear her purple skirt, and watch Barney), and letting her get up to her elbows in a sea of finger paints or, even better, bath paints.

child from falling into that gaping porcelain void? "Get a potty," says Ellen. "When toddlers sit on a potty, their feet are secure on the floor, and they aren't afraid of falling off." That's one opinion. Here's another: "Now that I have trained three, I will never go back to starting a young one on a potty chair again," says Dawn. "I just have those inserts right next to our toilets, and the kids think they are big stuff right from the start going on the big potty. I did this with my third one, and it went very smoothly. And you don't have to dump the potty into the big toilet, so it's just less mess." I'm with Dawn on this one. The less mess the better, in my book. And one way to solve the problem of dangling feet is to get a stool.

My Thirty-One-Month-Old

"Emma came out of the bathroom and came over to give me goodnight kisses, and her hair was wet. I asked her if she had touched her hair after washing her hands, to which she replied, 'No.' Completely horrified, I asked her how her hair got wet. 'I was looking at my poopy!' she said. We had started growing Emma's hair out, and she found out the hard way that she couldn't bend over as far to look in the toilet as she used to!" —Tonya

- *Whether you opt for the ring or the potty chair, allow your trainee to become familiar with the thing.* Let her look at it, touch it, and get comfy with it before attempting correct usage. Some potty pros even advocate nicknaming your potty, much like a pet. Gertrude. Appolonia. Serge. Whatever name you choose, try not to bust out laughing every time you say it, or the kid will know something is fishy with this whole "Spot the Potty" business. If your whimsy threshold is not quite so high—and mine is, if you must know—then simply try to get your child thinking that the potty is something special just for him. Decorate the thing with stickers or markers or make up ditties about how fab it is to use a toilet—whatever floats your boat.

- *Let your toddler sit on the potty fully clothed.* Get your child into a routine so it becomes normal to sit on the potty once a day. Let your child leave the potty at any time, and never force your child to spend time on the potty. She should never feel as if being on the potty is negative or any sort of punishment. After your little recruit is okay with sitting on the potty clothed, have her plop down unclothed. This will help her get used to the idea that one must—and this is key—undress before using the potty. "I've started putting Lily on the toilet whenever she's naked—before baths or while I'm dressing her," says Diana. "Although she'll sometimes go a little, she usually just gazes curiously into the bowl. In fact, one night this week she let just two drops spill into the toilet and then peed all over me as I was undressing her. But despite that one incident, I think she's getting the picture."

Quotable

"We had guests over when our seminaked, eighteen-month-old Georgia toddled into the room. I heard one my friends utter these now-immortal words: 'Where'd ya get that pine cone from, Georgie?' There was a brief uncertain silence and a heady stench in the air. It was not a pine cone."   —Peter Downey[1]

- *Some parents are huge advocates of letting their toilet draftees wallow in their own mess for a while:* "Let them get good and uncomfortable. Then maybe next time they'll think twice about what's going on in their bodies." I think this concept may work well for some and not at all for others. One camp opines that leaving tots in wet or soiled undies will only make the skin on their bottoms sore and red, which is counterproductive to the whole process, they say. The other group is adamant that toddlers need to get out of their comfort zones (that is, waterproof diapers) before any action will happen on the pot. One thing is true: Because modern diapers are designed to prevent any feeling of wetness, it may not be until she is diaper free that she can really make the link between wanting to pee and what the urge to pee feels like. You make the call if your munchkin responds better to one method or the other.

Hey, Whatever Works!

"My son Jay was trained during the summer when he was a few months past two. We said he could go potty in a bush if he wanted to, so he started peeing on bushes in our backyard when he needed to. Of course we had a few episodes where he relieved himself on trees at the playground, and one time he pooped on the deck, giving new meaning to the term *poop deck*. But other than that, he seemed to pick up on it rather quickly, and he soon figured out he could take this skill indoors to the potty."

—Ann

- *Once you think your cherub is ready, tell her that without diapers she will need to use the potty* (or "Petunia" if you've gone the cute route). Remind her throughout the day that she might like to use the potty. But don't let her sit on the potty until she says she does have to go. Otherwise she won't make the correlation for herself. How is this different from my mother's method, you ask, which involved dragging the kid off to do his business every hour on the hour whether he needed to or not? With all respect to your mother—and mine—this newer strategy helps the little one recognize her need to go. Ten minutes after saying, no, she's fine, she may realize she does have the urge to go. But that's okay because this way she isn't totally dependent on you to tell her. She may have that telltale "poop expression" on her face, sit on the toilet for half an hour, and immediately unload under the kitchen table when she gets off. Hey, keep your cool. It's all a lot of trial and error and, as writer Peter Downey says, "a matter of timing, patience, carpet shampoo and a good washing machine."[2]

- *You'll have to help with wiping afterward.* Show me a toddler who can swab his own deck properly, and I'll shake that little man's hand (no doubt after washed for twenty seconds with antibacterial soap). I find this very strange actually. They prepare you for changing diapers, but they never tell you about assisting with the cleanup of another non-baby-human-being's hindquarters. Or maybe I just wasn't listening. At any rate, it's gotta be done.

- *Break out the Bob the Builder briefs.* When the little man has graduated from potty intern to assistant producer, Potty Division, he should be using the potty several times a day and is probably ready for the thrill of underwear. Make a big production out of shopping for undies, and let your child choose his favorite motif. Kids groove on cool underwear, I'm telling you. When Jonah was a ring bearer at our former baby-sitter's wedding, he told anyone who would listen about his Spiderman underpants. It was the highlight of his day! Other rewards: M&M's, Skittles, gum— all of these have been used as compensation for proper toilet usage. Some experts say, though, that your happiness and excitement over his new accomplishment should be all the reward he needs.

Ten More Toilet-Teaching Tips to Keep in Mind

1. Moving, a new baby, and other transitions create stress in a toddler's life. Don't potty train during these times of flux, or you'll set yourself up for disaster.

2. Even if the kid is about to turn four, he's still within the normal range.

3. Toilet training is not a competition. Vanna White and Pat Sajack will not appear at your door with a selection of glamorous prizes if your kid beats your neighbor to wearing underwear.

4. When your child has a movement, have him watch you dump the stool into the toilet so you can make the connection clear: This is where these items go.

Voices: Tips from the Toddler Trenches

"We haven't gotten there with Willow yet, but with her eldest sister we learned the hard way. Since the two eldest were so close together, I was eager to get Caitlin potty trained. I cajoled and bribed. We sat in the bathroom and waited. It was very stressful for both of us. She just wasn't ready. So with the next two, I didn't do anything. I believed that when they were ready, they'd tell me, and they did. Meg was two or two and a half, and the toilet training was uneventful and *easy.* Haley took longer; she was closer to three. But as long as I wasn't uptight about it, it wasn't a problem. My neighbors made comments like, 'Aren't you ever going to potty train that girl?' to which I replied, 'No, I'm sure she'll be the only kid in kindergarten who still wears diapers!' I didn't care what others had to say; people will offer advice on everything. When Haley was ready, she just started using the potty. It was overnight and stress free. So much better than my experimentation on poor Caitlin."

—Traci

"I think potty training styles have a lot to do with the personality of the parents. I waited for my kids to show an interest and then went for it. It wasn't a pressure-thing for us. We definitely directed the

5. Don't use Pull-Ups if the signs of readiness are not there. They don't speed up potty training!

6. Applaud his successes and celebrate each achievement along the way. Praise your child for sitting on a potty, getting his pants on and off, and so on.

7. Use consistent lingo: If you say "pee pee" one day and "tinkle" the next, you'll confuse your child.

8. Some accidents are inevitable, but if your novice is truly ready

process, but we didn't make a big deal of getting it done within certain time constraints."

—Deone

"Potty training Amelia was easy! My husband, Rob, was the difficult one during that time. I started putting her on the toilet right away when she got up in the morning (she never did use the little potty that I bought her) and then returned her to a diaper. I asked her several times throughout the day if she had to pee or poop. Sometimes she did, sometimes she didn't. And sometimes she said she didn't when she really did. Then one day I asked her if she wanted to wear panties, and she said yes. From there on, she pretty much wore panties every day and a Pull-Up at night and during naps. That lasted about two months. Then she decided she didn't want a Pull-Up at night anymore. She wet the bed all of three times and has been great ever since. I think in total it took about six weeks from the first panty day until the last pee in bed. The trick is to potty train when children are ready and want to. If they don't want to, it'll never work. Lots and lots of hoots, hollers, and cheers when they use the toilet help too!"

—Laura

to manage without diapers, these should number very few. When accidents happen, gently remind him the mess is what a potty is for, change him, and make no fuss. Reacting negatively may make him resentful and less likely to try again.

9. If you are going crazy because your parents and in-laws are hounding you about potty training, skip to the next chapter.

10. Celebrate potty training by going out for dinner with your spouse. Toast the new groove at your house with a glass of dry white wine or sparkling cider—whatever flips your switch. Discuss how you're going to spend the $60 per month you had been spending on diapers on something fun and impractical!

Toy Story: Our Heroes and Role Models

At two and a half on the nose, Quentin ("Q") reveres his Uncle Ryan, a firefighter. All the live-long day he bugs his mom to read him stories about fire trucks, firedogs, and firefighters. His favorite toy is his Little People Fire Truck, which features a little plastic firefighter named Cheryl who blathers on about her job. Q loves to manipulate the hose on the truck and "spray" imaginary fires. For variety, Q's mom, Debbie, bought her son a toy doctor set with a stethoscope, thermometer, needle, and bandages. Guess what? Quentin couldn't have cared less about the doctor stuff. He just wanted to keep fighting fires. But that's just Quentin. A playmate could come over and find Q's doctor set utterly mesmerizing.

Tykes this age are starting to make sense of how the outside world works, and inventing scenarios for their toy bus drivers and police officers and farmers is great fun. Chunky, durable farms and dollhouses are therefore enticing playthings for toddlers. Playing with various figures, furniture, and rooms provides a springboard for little ones as they explore the relationships and roles they see around them.

More toys for the thirty- to thirty-two-month-old set:

- *Dolls and stuffed animals* with easy-to-fasten and easy-to-unfasten snaps, buttons, and zippers.
- *Simple jigsaw puzzles* for an absorbing challenge with a big payoff.

Fabulous Freebie: The Toilet Paper Tube. It's a telescope, a spyglass, a toilet paper tube! Yes, the humble TP tube can be anything your toddler's kaleidoscopic imagination makes of it. My boys have used this humble roll of cardboard for boats, cars, telescopes, totem poles, and, of course, weapons. Glue some tubes vertically into a shoebox and you've got a 3D cityscape. Affix some wagon-wheel pasta to a tube, slather some paint on it, and you've got a custom coupe your toddler will be busting his buttons over.

Cliffs Notes for the Commode, Cabin Fever, and Counting One, Two, Fweeee!

Your little angel is getting closer to his or her three-year-old birthday—and Grandma's getting nervous. "My friend Lorna from pinochle said her grandson was dry overnight by the time he was two," she reports, with a little edge to her voice. Oh brother, the pressure's really starting to build, isn't it? Try to remember who's the parent here—you!—and that times have changed since your mother-in-law had her twenty-month-old toilet phenoms dry as dustballs during the night. Don't panic. Here, I'll give you a rundown of the world-famous twenty-four-hour potty-training method, the difference between Mars and Venus on the potty, and a few clues for heading off Granny at the pass. Next, learn how to cope when the entire family is puking—except you—and then learn what to do when *you are* puking and the rest of the family is not. Though you'd think the process would be similar, it's actually quite different! And in this chapter's "Toy Story," begin to unravel the mysterious ways in which little kids crack the code of counting, not merely repeating you, but doing actual number crunching powered by their own gray matter!

Milemarker: Inquiring Minds Want to Know

Toddlers are inherently curious and understand much more than they can verbalize. Once their language skills start to blossom, they will pepper you with questions. "What that do?" "What's it raining, Mama?" And they love to take "why" as far as it will go: "Why is it snowing?"

Umm, I don't have a clue, you're thinking. So you make something up.
"To make the world look so pretty and clean and white."
"Why?"
"Because…well, it's cold outside, and snow goes with cold."
"Why?"
"Go ask Daddy." (Oy vey!)

Mars and Venus on the Potty

If you have a boy, as I do, you need to be wise to a few additional strategies. After all, different plumbing requires different methods. For one thing, boys are obsessed with their penis. My boys have been known to straddle, dip down at the waist, and gaze in admiration at their member. It's enough to completely boggle the female mind, this pride. But hey, what do I know?

The main potty-training difference between boys and girls is that boys have to learn to point that thing in the right direction. Aiming is hard, they tell me, and requires some practice. Because at first both genders are usually trained sitting down, you must teach your son to point his penis inside the potty for optimum results. He may sit down fast without checking and end up peeing outside the toilet—a depressing thing for all involved. Try to drill it into him that he must, must maneuver his member in the proper direction or all will be lost and he'll be in diapers until Grandma kidnaps him and trains him herself. Some trainers have found success with potty targets, such as Cheerios, smiley-faced toilet-paper squares, and store-bought bull's-eyes. I always let Doyle take over this whole dynamic of aiming and whatnot. He is a much better role model than I for this sort of thing.

Toilet Teaching, Part 2 (Or, All the Stuff That Got Left Out of Part 1!)

"Step One: Get a potty. Step Two: Explain to the child that Mommy and Daddy use a potty, and Big Bird uses a potty, and Barney uses a potty, and Vice-President Cheney uses a potty in an undisclosed location, and it's time for the child to start using the potty, so he or she can be a big boy or girl and everybody will be SO PROUD and it will be SO MUCH FUN! Step Three: Leave immediately on a 15-day business trip."

—Dave Barry[1]

There is much talk that girls train at an earlier age than boys. Do they? Statistically, yes, girls train an average of two to three months earlier than boys. Personally, I think this is because their parents *assume* girls will train earlier than boys and thus start the whole process sooner. At any rate, my friends and their children are all over the map as to whether their sons or daughters trained earlier. And my sister-in-law, who had all three boys in undies by their second birthday, struggled to train her fourth child, a girl, by the time she was three and a half. So that proves (unscientifically) to me that this boy/girl stuff is all a bunch of hooey. At least with girls, though, you don't have to tutor them in the fine art of aiming, and you don't have to disinfect the wall every time they go to the bathroom.

Twenty-Four Hours to a Drier You

Who wouldn't like to go from having to change diapers to having a dry, self-sufficient toddler in the mere space of twenty-four hours? That's why

Coming Up on Three

I found myself getting so sentimental when my baby started looking and acting like a little boy, which was a few months before his third birthday. Here's a letter I wrote to Jonah when he was about thirty-two months old:

Hey there, Jo Jo,

Everyone keeps saying we should write down all the cute stuff you say and do because we won't remember it someday when you're all grown up. You know I write for a job, so sometimes it is hard for me to write in my spare time. But I want to remember these precious times when you are in your soft plaid pajamas, and your feet are like pork chops with toes, and you can't sleep without your teddy bear, "Baby."

Well, let's see. What did we do today? It was Labor Day, and we were going to go sailing with Daddy's friend Len. But because of stormy weather, we just had a really nice day at home. I slept in late, which you know I love, and then we (you and I) covered the dining room table with an old sheet and just did our art stuff. You swirled your paintbrush in the water and smushed it on the paper. I tried to draw a giraffe, but it looked more like an ostrich. You wanted me to draw Grandpa Craker, so I gave it my best shot. You wanted to draw loops and squiggles with a black marker, so you did. I love that you enjoy paint and crayons and markers and stickers and Play-Doh! We have fun being creative, although I should do more with you. You played with Dinah, being sweet and silly with her. What was it you said the other day? I asked you about your gum, and you said it was gone. "In the river in my tongue," you said. You little goober! You swallowed your gum! Oh well, by the time you read this, it will be digested! Daddy canned pickles all day long. The whole house smells like apple-cider vinegar, and we have more pickles than McDonald's uses in a year. But your dad is happy that he is preserving the fruits of his garden.

We ordered a pizza (which you refused to eat; instead you wanted PB&J and candy, of course) and then watched *My Dog Skip,* which made Mommy cry and made Daddy scratch old Dinah behind the ears and talk baby talk to her. Daddy is tucking you in right now, and he's singing the Viking song from your current favorite book: *Hiccup the Seasick Viking.* You are giggling your little head off! Well, it's time for me and your baby sister or brother [Ez had not yet been born] to hit the sack. Hopefully you won't roll off the bed tonight like you did last night. Poor baby. I felt so bad for you. You are getting to be such a big boy, and I am so proud of you.

Love you,
Mama

the book *Toilet Training in Less Than a Day* by Nathan Azrin and Richard Foxx is a classic. Parents desperate for the magic potty formula grab the book off the shelf and practically run out the door with it. Later on you'll hear from a mom friend of mine who swears by the tenets in this little tome. For now, in case you have been living under a rock or haven't yet heard through the grapevine about these ideas, I will summarize them for you. Call it the Potty Seminar Cliffs Notes.

1. *Evacuate the home of all persons but trainer and trainee.* If anyone, let's say the child's father, for example, wants to hang around for the show, he must *fermer la bouche.* If Daddy "introduces a topic not relevant to the task of toileting," the authors write, ask Daddy to please retire to areas of the house not currently occupied by potentially toilet-trained individuals. If Daddy refuses, ask Daddy to please leave the building or go jump in the lake. (Why not have Daddy do the training and let Mommy go to the mall or something? Good question. This book is not exactly written from an equal-opportunity point of view.)

2. *Create a day spa in the kitchen.* "Training is usually conducted most conveniently in the kitchen," they opine. "The kitchen floor is usually designed to withstand spills or wettings, the necessary drinks can be kept cold, ice is available in the kitchen refrigerator, and a variety of snack items is usually stored there." Snacks are needed to demonstrate "your approval of the child for pottying correctly and for remaining dry."[2] Hey, it's a quote! Yeah, cold drinks and snacks are a big part of the M.O. here.

3. *Flood the kid.* "Drinks [should] be used as rewards…and will also serve to create a strong desire in your child to urinate, thereby providing many more urinations and more opportunities to teach your child how to potty correctly."[3]

4. *Bring on the dolls.* "A doll should be available at the start of training to serve as a model for demonstrating to your child the various steps of toileting correctly. The doll should be of the type that wets…and should wear training pants, so as to demonstrate the correct manner of lowering and raising them."[4] (I can just see Ezra flipping the doll over and demanding, "Where's her penis? Where's her penis?")

5. *Create a Friends-Who-Care list.* "When you will be praising your child during training, you will be telling him not only that you are pleased but also that others too will be pleased.… Make a list of the persons and friends your child admires, such as Daddy, his big brothers and sisters, his grandfather, his aunts, the mailman, and the baby-sitter. Also include fictional persons he admires, such as Santa Claus and the Flintstones…and the *Sesame Street* characters."[5] The book goes on to advise trainers to have letters of citation and congratulations available from these various individuals who "care" so much about the "toileting" process. Presumably, one would have to fictionalize letters from Fred and Wilma, Barney and Betty, Elmo, et al.

6. *Demonstrate.* After assembling all the necessary components, deluge the child with liquid as you demonstrate several times how the doll, once a diaper wearer, can now use the potty. Encourage the child to imitate the doll. At each moment of triumph, produce a lollipop or a message from Aunt Julia or from one of the Wiggles. Repeat as often as necessary until the child is potty trained. (Don't forget to call Daddy and tell him his period of exile has been lifted.)

I thought the whole thing sounded preposterous, but apparently I was wrong. Many, many people have met with resounding success using this one-day potty blitz. I was especially convinced by the following testimonial from my very savvy friend, fellow scribe, and literature professor Debra Rienstra:

When our daughter was a little younger than two, we found *Potty Training in Less Than a Day* and we thought, *Hey, that sounds good!* It's an old book, hopelessly sexist about parental roles, but the method in it was developed by two Ph.D.'s who wanted to help retarded adults learn to "potty themselves." We used their method, with some modifications, for our daughter, who made the switch out of diapers in one day at the age of twenty-five months. She had a few accidents the first couple weeks and needed help with the wiping business for a while. But she also was dry at night almost immediately. The grandparents absolutely couldn't believe it (that was the best part). When our second child came to his day of potty reckoning at thirty months, we braced ourselves, thinking that the first kid was maybe a fluke. But no—it worked for the second child, too. (He wasn't dry at night for a while, though.) Our third child was the hardest. He learned in one day all right. It just wasn't the day we chose. It was five days later, five days of many, many, many wet underpants. Still, I'd take five days of frustration over months of gradual learning. (Number Three was also dry at night right away.) No one, you'll be pleased to know, was emotionally scarred in the process. So I'm a firm believer in the intense propaganda campaign, followed by a one-day potty seminar, followed by a permanent switch out of diapers. I don't go for this "let him be in control" and "wait till he chooses to do it himself" stuff. He's two! He has no idea what he wants or what's best for him. The question is whether the child is physiologically and mentally ready. After that, there's nothing wrong with a little loving brainwashing to get the child's will on board with something everyone knows is the best thing.

Grandparents and Potty Training

In few areas does the generation gap seem to yawn as wide as it does in discussions of potty training. In the past, to escape the oppression of endlessly washing cloth diapers—I can just picture my mom doing exactly that with my brother's diapers!—toilet training began at a much earlier age. As I said in the previous chapter, my parents are now spreading the story that my own father was trained at ten months. When I pointed out that it wasn't even possible to teach a ten-month-old baby to use the potty, they shrugged their shoulders and said they were just repeating the story handed down by my grandmother, long since passed on. Hey, it's hard to argue with the dead, right? But there are plenty of folks from the early training generation who are still around and are eager as beavers to tell us all what we're doing wrong.

"If he can talk, he can be potty trained."

"Give her to me for a day, and she'll come home wearing panties!"

"Your sister and you were dry at fifteen months. Maybe you should take my little grandson to the doctor and see if there's anything wrong."

Sigh. It's enough to make a person run out and buy that peeing doll Azrin and Foxx are so crazy for. Sometimes the different points of view can cause some friction too. "With Avery, my mom asked me quite a few times when I would start potty training," says my friend Jane. "Her generation had kids off the bottle at age one and potty-trained at age two. Our generation is obviously more relaxed and has a 'wait until they're ready' approach. I think my mom eventually realized that my potty training philosophy was consistent with what today's pediatricians are recommending, so she laid off."

The old methods involved a lot of time watching one's child sit on the potties and waiting for release. There was a certain amount of victory in this approach, but it depended on parents making a potty available at the right time rather than on babies being able to control their bladders and bowels. I once heard it put like this: "Yes, toddlers used to be trained much sooner than they are today, but really it was the mommy who was trained and not the toddler." In other words, Mom had to be the one to nag and remind and predict when the child had to go to the bathroom and then to sit him on the pot and wait it out—ten times a day.

Call me crazy (or lazy), but constant surveillance and monitoring of a one-year-old's bathroom habits is not my idea of a good time. Nowadays most experts believe that toilet training, like many developmental achievements, should be "child centered," which means that we take our cue from the child rather than vice versa. Basically, we watch for the child to show that she's intrigued and wild about the idea before we broach toilet training.

My Thirty-Four-Month-Old

"We had a funny problem helping Amber adjust to her big-girl bed. We worried about losing the boundaries the crib offered, but our fears were unfounded: It never occurred to Amber that she could get out of bed on her own! She would drop her stuffed animal or blanket on the floor and call us to come pick it up. If she needed a drink of water, she'd call us to her room so she could tell us. When she woke early in the morning, it took several rounds of instruction to convince her she should play quietly in her room rather than hollering for us to see if she could get up yet. It was such an unexpected problem that (for the most part), it generated more laughs than annoyance."

—Erin

This strikes the older generation as very namby-pamby—like "Who's in charge around here anyway?" They don't see why we have to do things differently. After all, look how we turned out! If your tot's grandfolks are fussing over the fact that he's not trained yet, try to deflect the criticism with some humor: "Hey, don't worry, Mom. They are making diapers bigger and bigger all the time."

However, if the AARP people in your lives are really making a commotion about it in front of your little sweetie, it's time to have a little chat:

"You guys did a great job raising—and toilet training—Bob, obviously. Now it's time for us to do things our way. Hopefully we'll learn from our mistakes just as you did." Or, "Our pediatrician says thirty-six months is well within the range of normal for potty training. Katie seems more interested lately, so I'm sure she'll be trained soon."

Have the grandparents been badgering your child or even scolding him when he has an accident? Yikes! It's time for No More Missus Nice Guy. Decompress and gain some calm before you confront them, but also let them know you don't want them shaming your little one for a potty mishap because their criticism will just make things worse.

If your parents or in-laws just won't back down and your toddler does have a loving relationship with them, call their bluff and let them try their hand at potty training. Knock yourself out, Granny! It may sound preposterous, but experts say that since your toddler won't have the same kinds of rebellion issues with his grandparents as he has with you, he may give them a much easier time. As long as you feel comfortable with the general approach your child's grandparents are planning to take, it's reasonable to let them start potty training, even if you'd planned to wait a little longer. However, consistency is important for toddlers, so it's important to get everyone on the same page before you begin. (And of course this all hinges on your relationship with your parents and in-laws. A testy relationship probably won't be improved if Granny is lording over you her success in potty training your child!)

TV Nation

Maybe because I'm an entertainment writer, I don't happen to think television is the root of all evil. When we were little chicks, you and I, about all we could watch was *Sesame Street*. Now of course there are dozens of shows for toddlers and preschoolers, and most of them are quite good. The rule of thumb, they say (you know, "They," that panel of anonymous experts that dictates good choices for the universe at large), is about half an hour for every year of life, capping it off at about an hour and a half or two hours at age four. Some of the new shows, such as *Dora the Explorer,* even teach some second-language skills—which will lead an Anglo like my Ez to walk around saying, *Hola!* I say, give yourself a break and let your toddler watch a couple of quality shows if he wants to. You pour so much of yourself into raising your toddler, and I think you deserve a break! (And so do I for that matter!) Here are some of my fave television shows for tots:

- *Dora the Explorer* (Interactive!)
- *The Wiggles* (Get up and "Do the Monkey"!)
- *Blue's Clues* (It's too much fun to watch your little person holler out answers! They must think Joe is a moron!)
- *Jay Jay the Jet Plane* (Includes character-building themes.)
- *Clifford the Big Red Dog* (Cute—and the kiddies lap it up!)

Diary of a Woman Trapped in a House with a Squirting Toddler (a.k.a.: Sick Munchkin)

We've just had a week here at the Craker ranch so fraught with intestinal disasters, runny noses, and burning foreheads that it really should have been documented by the National Geographic Society ("New and Virulent Bacteria Runs Rampant in Midwestern Family"). Though I bleached the countertops, sprayed doorknobs with Lysol, pushed vitamins like some kind of drug dealer, still it happened: My children got sick. Again. There was some kind of nasty bug going around, or so the overburdened doctor's office reported when I dragged my malaise-ridden youngsters in for a look-see.

Jonah threw up almost around the clock at the beginning of the week. Whew! Thank goodness that part was over. But then the diarrhea started, which was worse, much worse, at least in terms of messes to clean up. I lived in mortal fear that Ezra would also begin the horrible cycle, but he had another germ entirely to contend with. While one kid raced to the toilet every half hour (and made it only about half the time), the other kid was hot and listless, wanting to be held continuously. Why did we have two kids, I wondered, when plainly we could only handle one flu bug at a time, and, even more plainly, flu bugs come in groups? I craved sleep in a way I hadn't since my babies were small. That's one thing they don't tell you when you sign up for this parenthood thing: Sleep deprivation is forever.

But you and I both know what the worst thing about sick kids is—hands down—CABIN FEVER. It's usually up to Mom to hang with her afflicted posse, administering medicine, cleaning messes, changing sheets (try cleaning up or changing sheets with a screaming toddler clamped to your leg), and generally trying to emanate a soothing, nurselike presence. The minutes tick by as you wait for your husband to come relieve you. (And if you have no husband or if your husband is out of town all the time, my compassion for you is boundless!) If your home has been a sick bay for a few days, it's safe to say the walls are closing in, and you're about ready to jump in a snowbank head first.

Some people are much more suited to being trapped in their homes with sniffling, hacking little ones than others. I am not at all suited to this. In fact, I find it more tortuous than getting sick myself, because when I'm

Faith Builder

When your squirtie or you are feeling green around the gills, what better time to rely on the Great Physician for strength, healing, and comfort? Give your toddlers extra TLC, of course, and underscore the fact of God's love and care by adding that God wants them to feel better too. Pray specifically to make the ouchie—or whatever it is that's gone awry in your family's immune system—go away![6]

sick, I don't feel like going out! But I'll tell you, on these miserable occasions, even a run to the corner store for diapers can feel like some kind of spa experience.

Your husband is your number-one ally in helping you stay sane during times like these. Maybe, like Doyle, your partner could (once in a blue moon) use his sick benefits to come home and take care of the kids while you escape. Lots of companies design sick days to incorporate not only the employee's sickness but also their family members' illnesses, too. A husband's use of a personal day is also a possibility, although he probably gets only a few each year. If Dad's coming home for a full or partial day isn't an option, then when he actually does finish his workday, by all means turn the shift over to him. I mean, trample the man if you must, but get out of Dodge when he comes home! Go out for coffee by yourself or with a buddy. Hit the library or the mall. Or do something mundane but utterly beautiful, like getting the car washed or doing some grocery shopping. These little nighttime breaks will fuel your nursing tank and give you a key change of scenery. After an hour or two out of the infirmary, you'll be ready again to wipe noses, hold a fussy toddler, and do laundry, laundry, laundry!

Diary of a Woman Too Ill to Realize She's Watched "Elmopalooza" Twelve Times (a.k.a.: Sick Mommy)

"Ask any mom what the worst part of staying at home is," says writer Allie Pleiter, "and you'll probably get the same answer: being sick while you're still trying to take care of children. It's hard to decide which is worse: taking care of sick kids while you're sick too, or trying to deal with healthy kids while you're on your deathbed. Both are particular tortures of motherhood."[7]

Allie goes on to describe the heart-melting moment when, decimated by a headache, she watched her two-year-old, Christopher, toddle over to her bearing his very own special blankies. "Okay now, Mama," he said as he crammed the blankets into his mommy's arms, sealing the whole TLC moment with a mushy kiss on her forehead. Awww. That's so sweet! Christopher's act of compassion blessed her socks off and proved more curative than painkillers.

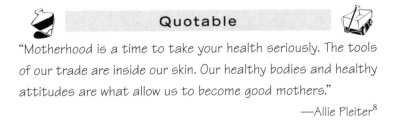

Quotable

"Motherhood is a time to take your health seriously. The tools of our trade are inside our skin. Our healthy bodies and healthy attitudes are what allow us to become good mothers."

—Allie Pleiter[8]

Allie has some nifty ideas for "Chief Home Officer" sick-day benefits. She and a close buddy have made a sick-day pact. When Allie is too sick to care for her own children, she calls her friend for help. And the next time her friend comes down with bubonic plague, Allie returns the favor. Here are a few more survival helps from Allie and me:

- *Bless the VCR.* "[Sick days] are exactly why God invented the VCR," Allie says. Feel abundantly free to pop in an extended-play tape and let your turbo-toddler be a couch potato all day long if you need to. Now's not the time to feel guilty for letting your child watch too much television. When you're so achy you feel as if you may have somehow contracted dengue fever, the "bone-cracking" fever of the Amazon, *you need to lie down!* You're not a bad mommy if, on a sick day, you forgo the daily craft hour to cop some much needed recuperation—and if you're gluing Popsicle sticks together anyway, you're not that sick.

- *Gather your Sick Squad.* "Few tortures are worse in this life than clinging to the pharmacy counter, trying not to throw up, waiting for your prescription while your toddler is busy rearranging the toothpaste aisle," Allie writes.[9] Find a pharmacist who delivers or, failing that, one who has a nifty drive-through window. Who wants to bundle up a feverish eighteen-month-old in the dead of winter and wait in a long line for your prescription? Not *moi!* Some grocery stores deliver too, which is a bonus and a half when you're sneezing so often your two-year-old can accurately pronounce "gesundheit," yet the only food left in the house belongs to the gerbil. Ah-choo at the delivery guy if you must, but at least you'll have some vittles to throw at the kids.

- *A pound of prevention.* I've always been one to catch the bug du jour. Now that I'm a mom, though, it's infinitely harder to just crash in bed and wake up a few days later. Actually, it's impossible unless I can time my head colds and flus for weekends when Doyle is home and we have nothing going on! Over the years I've developed a strategy for fending off most germy attackers. When I feel that portentous, here-we-go-again thing creeping through my cells—for me, that's an achy, blechy feeling, the beginnings of a sore throat, and a "swimmy" head—I take immediate action. Popping vitamin C in any form helps, and most times a shot up the nose of this newfangled nasal gel stuff—proven to kill the bug where it originates, in your nasal passages—works wonders. If possible I hit the sack hard for a solid eleven to twelve hours of restorative sleep. Experts say a marathon snooze session can ward off a full-blown bubonic plague. I also pop some cold meds before I sleep. This action plan may sound extreme—who wants to squirt anything in her nostrils, and who has time to sleep that much?—but I'm telling you, it beats the ol' four-day flu. Of course, if you're nursing or pregnant, talk to your doc about what over-the-counter meds are okay for you in your efforts to stave off the worst.

Toy Story: Who Said Math Can't Be Fun?

She's almost three, and Vivienne knows it. "I'm freeeeee!" she'll jubilantly declare to anyone who will listen. She's so excited about being "free" she can almost taste the frosting on her cake. "How many fingers are you?" mom Wanda will ask, coaxing her little princess to show the world how advanced she is. Vivi will obediently hold up three nubby little fingers, proudly showing off her ability to count to three. But can she really count to three, or is she just parroting what Mommy and Daddy have told her about how old she is? Vivienne might actually have the brainpower to count to three, but more likely she's just repeating the word around town, which is that she is soon to be no longer two.

So what's the big deal? Kids younger than Vivi have counted to ten, no problem. But experts say there is a distinction between repeating a familiar chain of sounds—"Say, 'One, two, three, four, five,' sweetie"— and actually "cracking the code" of counting and grasping what the numbers mean. Ezra could recite his numbers pretty well, but one day he took a group of candles out of a basket, looked it over, and said, "Fwee candles, Mommy!" I wish I had known what an accomplishment that really was— I might have let him play with those candles a little longer!

During playtime you can help your toddler understand the concept of groups or patterns of things. Take two cars and say, "How many cars are there?" If he says, "Two," you'll know he really gets it. Build slowly, adding a toy to the pile. Use a type of plaything your little dude really gets jazzed about. Ezra adores plastic animals of any kind. His favorite thing to do when we visit Jonah's preschool is to take all the plastic zoo animals out of the bin and arrange them to his liking. Sometimes I'll sort the animals in pairs—this is a great Noah's ark–related game—and see if he can start to see the pattern. Most of the time I just let him loose in his own glorious imaginary world of play. (Amazingly enough, "Math time with Mommy" gets old pretty quick. Go figure.)

Here's one more way to reinforce numbers: Buy some of those foam letters and numbers that stick onto the bathtub. After a few rounds of fun with "that little fellow who's cute and yellow and chubby," talk about the numbers on the tub and what they represent: "There are two duckies in your tub, honey. And three boats. One, two, three. See, that's the number three, right there by your foot!" Of course, when you're teaching any concept to two-year-olds, an inordinate amount of enthusiasm is necessary. Gush about numbers as if they are the greatest thing since bubble bath, and chances are Junior will soak it up.

More choices for a ducky playtime:

- *Large, magnetic letters and numbers* for the fridge.
- *Finger puppets.* (Uber-cute, finger puppets do tend to disappear into that great quagmire of socks, puzzle pieces, and small toys that exists in every home. Keep a vice grip on the little critters, though, and you'll have a theatrical, imaginative activity at your fingertips.)

Fabulous Freebie: Twist and Shout. Pipe cleaners are colorful, malleable, and dirt cheap. They don't even crumble and get mashed into the carpet like Play-Doh. Demonstrate how to twist and loop pipe cleaners into shapes and see what your novice artist makes of them. Jonah and I made a legion of spiders when he was almost three. And because his buddy Nathan had glasses—an accessory Jonah dearly coveted for himself—I made him a few pairs of pipe-cleaner glasses that actually outlasted his urge for specs. People craftier than I will have other ideas on what can be done with pipe cleaners, so by all means consult them. (Try FamilyFun.com!)

Self-Care Sanity Savers, Spiritual Foundations, and Swell Duds

Here we are, fellow moms, at the end of this demanding, intense, and beautiful passage called toddlerhood. You've seen a teetering one-year-old grow into a boisterous, chattering little person of three years—unbelievable! With their enormous energy, expansive love, and their flinty, strong wills, my two sons were prime examples of turbo-toddlers. I know I sometimes wondered if I would survive the tantrums, the constant testing, and the basic mulishness. But I also look back with a special fondness on the terrain our family traversed from the boys' babyhood to childhood. The toddler years are forever etched in our memories exactly because they were so challenging, but the payoff is that anything you're so deeply invested in becomes truly precious. I hope you'll come away from reading this final chapter knowing how to truly enjoy your toddler—not simply surviving until he or she turns three but actually delighting in this child you've been given the privilege of rearing.

Though I've scattered "Faith Builders" throughout this book, I've devoted much of this chapter to imparting a spiritual life to your little one. First I share some of my ideas, and then my faithful posse of friends—moms in the toddler trenches like you—give their best examples of passing on a legacy of belief. I think their Christmas and Easter tips are especially fantastic! And finally, in the last but not least "Toy Story" section, get in touch with your inner drama queen when we open the "tickle trunk" for dress-up fun.

Milemarker: Those Awful Night Terrors

Has your usually great sleeper been waking in the night, crying? Right around now some toddlers start experiencing night terrors, which are most common between the ages of three and five. If yours is simply tearful and upset, she could be having a nightmare or possibly a little bout of separation anxiety. But if she can't be comforted or stares right through you, she's probably having night terrors. These often occur when Little Miss wakes from deep sleep. Your tot may seem muddled and confused, or she might even push you away. Try to stay calm and wait for her to sleep again. In the morning she won't even remember what happened.

How to Really Enjoy Your Toddler

No question, raising a turbo-toddler is a taxing endeavor. Basic care and feeding of the munchkin is enough to make your motherhood plate full, but throw in whining, tantrums, defiance, and the never-ending need to avert disaster, and you can feel overwhelmed. I know some days I felt—and feel—completely demented by all the demands.

Even so there are surprising pleasures in this job of bringing up a food-flinging darling. You may even, like me, shock yourself when one day, when your little person is speaking in complete sentences and lugging a backpack to preschool, you find you miss your irascible toddler. Enjoy these post-baby, pre-kid days. But when you're still in the trenches and find yourself in nurture shock, it's key for you to regain your equilibrium and refuel your own energies and passions. Here are a few methods that will help you avoid toddler-care burnout. If you're successful in taking care of yourself, you'll be able to stop and smell the dandelions, not just trample them underfoot. Be intentional about taking pleasure in this fleeting, often turbulent passage. I guarantee you the journey will be sweeter.

- *Remember who you were a mere thousand days ago* when potty training was the last thing on your mind. Try to recapture some of your old interests, whether they include a regular Pilates class or going to a blues festival or the beach. (My hairdresser takes off one day a year to hit the beach with her girlfriend. They bake in the sun for hours, reading glossy magazines with no articles about teething or tantrums. Peggy comes back rejuvenated and restored.) Trade time off with your husband to pursue an old passion (as in hobby, not the guy who broke your heart in college. Just so we're clear.)

My Thirty-Six-Month-Old

"Ivy now has an imaginary friend named Oswald, which I think must be after the octopus on that TV show. She'll say, 'Oswald's at the door, Mommy,' and she'll run to the door and greet him. Ivy tried to pull this little trick where she said, 'Oswald doesn't have to sit in a car seat anymore,' hoping I would let her get away without buckling in to hers. I just said, 'Oswald's mommy would want him to be safe, so I think we should buckle him in. Will you help him?' It worked so well that I sometimes use good ol' Oswald to my advantage."   —Jennifer

- *Cut yourself some slack.* It ain't easy, but try not to let guilt—that bane of motherhood—capsize your mental state. Sure, you gave the kid sugary cereal, you caved in at the grocery store and bought him a sucker, and you yelled at him and made him cry when he scribbled purple marker on the coffee table. We've all been there. Ask God to forgive you and to give you a fresh start. If you need to, ask your toddler to forgive you and then start over with him, too. Take a deep breath and remember you're a good mom even though you make mistakes.

- *Join a moms' group like MOPS.* Hanging out with like-minded moms who often experience the same "he flushed my watch down the toilet" woes as you can really lighten your load. Find support, be encouraged, eat a cookie, and make a picture frame. It's all good.

- *"Trust yourself,"* says Dr. Spock in the first line of his classic manual of childcare. "You know more than you think you do." By now you've been able to concoct your own philosophy of child rearing. You've used a measure of instinct, some common sense, lots of trial and error, and a pinch of individuality that gives your family savor. Credit yourself for the things you do well and try not to compare yourself to the apparently perfect mommy down the block (she who vacuums in pearls and high heels). "Raising a child is not a paint-by-numbers kit," says writer Paula Spencer. "It's more like piecing together a quilt, stitching together random bits of silk, velvet, and wool in ways that look right to you."[1]

- *When in doubt, look to the hills!* That's where your help is gonna come from. I couldn't last a day with my turbo-tot without my God to rely on for wisdom, courage, comfort, and stamina. "Lord, just get me through this day," you pray. And He always does.

- *Relax!* Toddlers are fun, remember? Well, at least sometimes they are fun. Hold on to your sense of humor when the going gets tough, and loosen up whenever you can. Hey, look at it this way —that child of yours is almost three years old. You got her this far, so you may as well keep going! Besides, you have a birthday cake to bake (or order, as it were). Your child's third birthday is truly a milestone not only for her but for you, too. Feel pride in your accomplishment—and take lots of pictures!

Toddlers and Spirituality

Here are some ways to impart the essence and vitality of faith to your toddler:

- *Introduce spirituality early.* "Young children don't understand who God is, but they don't really understand who a grandparent is either," says Dr. Marianne Neifert. "Still, you want them to know Grandma, so you start talking about her from day one. It's the same thing with the idea of God." Just as your child takes your word for it that Grandma is an important person in her life (even if she rarely sees her), so she'll take your word for it that God is important too. Also, if you introduce spiritual practices early on— such as lighting candles or singing hymns together—your child will view them as a natural part of life, and you'll have a spiritual influence on her before other people do.[2]

       Words to Live By

"Hear, O Israel: The LORD our God, the LORD is one. Love the LORD your God with all your heart and with all your soul and with all your strength. These commandments that I give you today are to be upon your hearts. Impress them on your children. Talk about them when you sit at home and when you walk along the road, when you lie down and when you get up. Tie them as symbols on your hands and bind them on your foreheads. Write them on the doorframes of your houses and on your gates."   Deuteronomy 6:4-9

- *Create a "blessing book."* Buy either some kind of a keepsake journal or a formal book such as *My Son's Blessing Book* or *My Daughter's Blessing Book* (WaterBrook Press) to record your affirmations of love and to bless your child as only his mom and dad can. "If we were to do so," reads the introduction to *My Son's Blessing Book*, "we would create a permanent testament for our son to keep, a personalized record of our love and God's as it applies to the details of his existence, a documentation of the physical and spiritual heritage that has unfolded in his life. Whatever might happen to us, whatever route his life would take, he would always have it. He would always be able to read it, always be encouraged by it, ever pointed back, as if by a compass, to the love of Christ and his Father's perfect Word."[3] Erin and her husband, Tim, have created a similar book—a collection of letters written to their daughter on each of her birthdays. "Amber won't read these letters for years to come," says Erin. "We'll give the book to her on an as-yet-undecided significant birthday (thirteen, sixteen, eighteen?). And the letters will provide an important written record of our love and prayers for her, especially should something happen to either or both of us before she reaches adulthood."

- *Build on family traditions.* Spirituality not only links us to heaven, but it also connects us to one another and to the past. If you're raising your child in the same spiritual tradition that you were raised in, be sure she knows that these beliefs and practices were passed along by her grandparents and even her great-grandparents. I have some black-and-white photos of my Grandpa Loewen, a devout, salt-of-the-earth wheat farmer, reading his Bible. An uncle had this portrait of faith enlarged to a five-by-seven, so whoever is looking at the picture can see both the intent look on Grandpa's face and his work-worn hands touching the well-used binding. This photo reminds me of my kind grandpa and, more important, of his reverence for the Scriptures. When I show my boys their great-grandfather reading his Bible, they get to know something of who he was, and they gain a greater sense of the heritage of faith that Grandpa passed to my mom, my mom passed to me, and I'm passing to them. We also talk to our children regularly about the core values of their forebears: "Grandma Finney loved Jesus, and now she's with him in heaven"; "Grandma Loewen loved this song. It reminded her of how much God loved her"; and "Old Oma was a very brave lady. She escaped from bad men during the war. Many times she didn't have enough to eat or even a dry place to sleep. But she relied on God to help her." By the time Jonah was a preschooler, he had absorbed these details from the family storybook. Visiting "Old Oma" (my one-hundred-year-old grandmother) in the nursing home then became a treat, a precious opportunity to spend time with this brave woman to whom he was related. Don't underestimate how much your toddler can soak in. Keep it simple, true, and relevant, and she'll surprise you with how much she understands about her spiritual heritage.

 Quotable

"Remember that no matter how active, curious, difficult or infuriating your toddler seems at times, it's all a dress rehearsal for the real world. Consider yourself her first acting coach, director, and most adoring audience."   —Tracy Hogg[4]

- *Make it fun.* Spirituality should be joy-filled and creative, not a legalistic drag. Encourage your toddler to paint a picture of God or heaven. Act out plays together, like Noah's ark using plastic animals, or put on puppet shows based on other Bible stories and spiritual themes such as kindness and joy. Above all, do what spiritual people have done for centuries—sing and dance!
- *Introduce a simple form of prayer.* Let your child know that prayer isn't something that's saved for Sunday morning or for times when she needs help with something. Prayer is a tool for communicating

with God anytime. Demonstrate that spirituality is a part of everyday life by incorporating it into ordinary actions and words. Invite your little one to join you in saying a prayer at different times of the day—for example, when she sees something beautiful or when she does something for the first time. Your prayers can be simple: "Let's pray and ask Jesus to help Opa be brave for his time at the hospital"; "Thank you, God, for helping Mommy find her keys!"; and "God made this caterpillar. Isn't that awesome? Let's tell Him thank You." The idea is to let your child know that God is always available for them.

- *Nurture your toddler's natural compassion.* Some children this age are very sensitive to the pain of others. They might worry about a baby who is crying or whether someone who gets hurt is going to be okay. Many toddlers are also fascinated with sirens or emergency vehicles. Use their budding compassion as an opportunity to pray for other people whenever you notice the need—when the ambulance howls by on the street, when you hear an unhappy baby in the supermarket, and so on. Even if you don't know what is wrong, you and your little prayer warrior can ask God to take care of the people involved and to soothe their hurts.

- *Establish routines.* Pray regularly when your toddler wakes up or goes to bed. A simple prayer of thanks before or after meals can be an easy and effective way to instill appreciation for the basics of life. We do a mealtime prayer that goes like this: "God made the sun. God made the sea. God made the fishes. God made me. Thank You for the sun. Thank You for the sea. Thank You for the fishes. And thank You for me." Ezra loves the hand motions of the sun and the sea, and he is absolutely insistent on praying this prayer! If your child is too young to make up her own prayers, help her along with what Neifert calls "Ping-Pong" prayers: You suggest a simple phrase like "Thank You, God, for…," and she fills in the blank.

Voices: Words on Faith

In the Daily Stuff of Life…

"I sing 'Jesus Loves Me' to Adam every night, and we say a little bed-time prayer. Our prayers are nothing formal, just a little rundown of our day—giving thanks and then asking for help with our challenges, for good health, and for a good night's sleep. I worry a lot about keeping Adam safe in this world. Then I realized that I, as an 'earthly' parent, cannot be with Adam every moment of every day of his life, but his 'heavenly' parent can be and will be. So I pray every night for God to keep Adam safe."

—Ann

"When Max was between the ages of one and two, we'd all lie on the living room floor. He'd be drinking a bottle, and Rick or I would read from *Baby's First Bible* (Standard Publishing). Those were cozy, special times. I think it is so amazing to be able to tell our kids about God as a normal part of life. Sometimes it amazes me that they are actually learning the fundamentals of Christianity at such an early age. When both boys were around eight months old and in a high-chair, we would gently put their little hands together and say, 'Let's pray.' Then we'd simply say, 'Thank You, Jesus, for the food.'

"A few months ago we were sitting down at the table to eat at our friends' house—their boys are basically the same ages as ours. You know how it is with the noise and excitement of being able to sit together while eating, so it was noisy at the table. But when Don said, 'Let's pray,' everything was quiet, we all bowed our heads, and he said grace. After the 'amen,' the chatter began again. Juanita pointed out how it was so natural and automatic for their kids and ours to thank the Lord for the food before eating. I loved that observation."

(continued)

"In our home we also try to remember to pray for safety, for wisdom in what we buy and how we spend our money, and for help finding what we need when we make our one-hour trek to the grocery store. Throughout the day, whenever any concern comes up (illness, death, missionaries—anything) throughout the day, we stop what we're doing and pray about it. It's something we *really* want our kids to learn and begin to experience for themselves, that *God always cares and always listens,* and whatever matters to us, matters to Him, too."

—Alanna

"As for faith and toddlers, you just have to live it. We pray at mealtime. They catch on. I do try to read them lots of Bible stories, and we have quite a collection now. For a while, when I was reading three stories to Nathanael before nap and three before bed, I always made sure the last one was a Bible story. We have a couple of devotionals for kids that make them answer questions about the story. I like that one because it made Nathanael think. I'm not as good about that now as I used to be. There always seems to be room for improvement here. Other than that, we just try to talk about Jesus when we can, like I ask what the story was in nursery. I really would like to work more on Bible verse memory with them too."

—Cheryl

"My very good friend Carla Williams created a 'Quiet Time Box' for her three sons (all grown now), and she made one for me as a baby-shower gift when I was expecting Amber. The box is a storage box that contains a variety of toys and books that Mom or Dad can pull out and use as soon as Baby is old enough to sit up (about six months). The box comes out to help the kids enjoy their own focused Bible times (starting at about ten minutes in length and increasing as your child gets older). Each story or toy has a simple

Sunday-school song to go with it. For example, a storybook of numbers goes with a song about what God created on each day: 'Day one, day one, God made light when there was none...' A small collection of toy animals goes with the song: 'I'm a little old cow (pig, sheep, duck, and so on), and God made me, I'm as happy as I can be. God the Father made the cow to say, "Mooooo."' A board book of fruits and vegetables teaches that God made good food for us to eat. Teething rings shaped like a foot or hand teach that God made us. Flannel figures of ethnically diverse figures teach that God made each of us special: Sing 'Jesus Loves the Little Children.' The New Testament teaches us about Jesus and God's love for us: Your toddler looks in a handheld mirror and sings 'Jesus Loves Me.' Parents can create their own Quiet Time Box with toys from a dollar store and favorite Sunday-school songs. The truly creative can write their own lyrics to popular nursery songs. And for those of us who don't like to sing (I'm no good at it!), there are plenty of good Christian audiotapes to choose from."

—Erin

During the Holidays...

"The Nativity scene is the focal point of our decorating for the holidays. Since the Wise Men traveled far to see the baby Jesus, we start the Wise Men out in the back of the house in separate locations. Each morning our two-year-old daughter eagerly moves the Wise Men closer to Jesus. On Christmas morning, before we open presents, our daughter happily allows the Wise Men to sit by the stable. This provides an opportunity each morning to talk about the story of this blessed birth."

—Abby
(continued)

"During Advent we tried to do devotions after dinner and light the candles and all that, but Adam didn't want to sit still for it. So we bagged it for this year. I heard about a great book at MOPS called *The Advent Book.* It's like an open-the-flap book with one page for each day of Advent. I think I will feel more comfortable with a toddler and an interactive book than with a toddler attempting to be interactive with lighted candles."

—Ann

"For Christmas we took the boys to go and look at Santa. They had no desire to sit on his lap, nor did we feel they had to have a picture with him. We know that Santa is very 'there,' but we explain to them that he is a dressed-up man and that Mommy and Daddy and other people we love give us presents, not Santa. Really, God is the *only* one who 'knows when you are sleeping...knows when you're awake... knows if you've been bad or good,' *not* Santa. We definitely listen to Christmas songs that sing about Santa. We don't portray Santa as evil or sinful, but we emphasize that Christmas is about Jesus' birthday. We don't do Santa decorations or Santa wrapping paper. But, unlike my parents, I don't scowl and make it all 'evil'!

"Sometimes I feel that's what my parents did—make all the 'worldly things' (Christmas trees and lights on the house, bunnies and baskets at Easter) seem so wrong. I know these are not the true reasons for celebrating, but now I make sure that my place looks very Christmasy."

—Alanna

"As for Christmas and Easter, we haven't said that Santa and the Easter Bunny don't exist, but we don't go out of our way to promote them either. (Our children do get a stocking and an Easter basket, though.) I really make an effort to have lots of Christmas and Easter books that are about Christ. For Advent we light the candles at dinner and sing 'Come Thou Long Expected Jesus' every night after we eat. They really enjoy that. I also have two kid-friendly Nativity sets that we encourage them to play with."

—Cheryl

"We bought our daughter, Amber, her very own Nativity set when she was three. It's a tiny set made of impossible-to-break resin figures small enough for her to handle but not choke on. I've seen similar child-friendly sets made of plastic or wood. We told Amber the Christmas story using the figures and let her have free rein in playing with the set—and she loved it. She especially responded to the idea that Jesus was a baby. There's a wonderful little picture book called *The Nativity* by Julie Vivas, the text of which is drawn directly from the King James, that Amber just loves. We read it year-round—not just at Christmas. The watercolor illustrations are charming, and Amber likes to look at the book on her own even though she can't read yet."

—Erin

"For Easter we made a lamb out of a paper plate and some cotton balls, then added a verse to it about Jesus being our Good Shepherd. I also printed some Eastery clip art off the Internet and wrote a verse reference on the back of each small piece of art. I then placed each inside a plastic egg. We opened one each night the week or so before Easter. While Jody or I read the pertinent Easter-related verses, Nathan colored the Easter art. Each night we added the art to a sort of Easter garland, which grew through the week."

—Laura

We've talked at length in this book about the many joys and challenges of raising these capricious, sweet, adorable, pint-sized people we call toddlers. At the beginning of toddlerhood, they still bore many of the markings of babyhood—clinging, learning to walk, babbling. Two years later, you know your little one so much better, and you've prepared him to walk a new path: the path of childhood. Soon the baby days will be a distant memory, and the infants of yesterday will be the little men and little women of tomorrow. (Kinda makes you just want to cry your eyes out, doesn't it?) As you come to your toddler's third birthday, the official passage from baby days into the world of a child, be sure you are laying a solid spiritual foundation for your child and nurturing him in the ways of the One who loves him even more than you do.

Toy Story:
The Tickle Trunk

Every Canadian child remembers Mr. Dress-Up, our own dear, dear television friend, and the hours of play he initiated with his hallmark "tickle trunk," a magical trunk filled with dress-up clothes. Some of my friends in Canada have passed this tradition on to their little Canucks, creating "tickle trunks" of their own. Of course Yankee children will also benefit from the imagination-sparking of a costume box! Fill a large rubber container (or an old clothes hamper, like I had) with your fancy hand-me-downs. (You know, the glittery purple dress? It was hideous as a bridesmaid's gown, but hem it with duct tape and it will be glamorous fun for your girl.) Also, check out specialty catalogs for all kinds of pint-sized costumes: firefighters, police officers, knights, superheroes, princesses, and animals. My guys have gorilla costumes that are just too cute.

Dress-up clothes encourage little ones to broaden their horizons and think creatively about who they want to pretend to be. If your junior Lancelot starts weaving a tale about his adventure, put it down on paper and read it to him later. You'll be modeling a key literacy concept: how marvelous and fulfilling it can be to come up with ideas and express them through reading and writing.

Notes

2: Fourteen to Sixteen Months

1. Beth Kephart, "How Children Learn to Talk," *Parenting*, March 2003, 87.
2. "It Worked for Me," *Parents*, November 2002, 46.
3. "Ages and Stages: 1 to 2," *Parenting*, March 2003, 162.
4. Vicki Iovine, *The Girlfriends' Guide to Toddlers* (New York: Perigree, 1999), 7.
5. T. Berry Brazelton, M.D., *Touchpoints: The Essential Reference: Your Child's Emotional and Behavioral Development* (New York: Perseus, 1992), 392.

3: Sixteen to Eighteen Months

1. John Trent, Ph.D., Rick Osborne, and Kurt Bruner, general editors, *Parents' Guide to the Spiritual Growth of Children* (Wheaton: Tyndale, 2000), 115.
2. Sal Severe, as quoted by Liz Rusch in "Make No Mean No," *Parents*, November 2002, 214.

4: Eighteen to Twenty Months

1. "It Worked for Me," *Parents*, November 2002, 46.

5: Twenty to Twenty-Two Months

1. Arlene Eisenberg, et al., *What to Expect the Toddler Years* (New York: Workman, 1996), 215.
2. Michelle Kennedy, *Eating: 99 Tips to Bring You Back from the End of Your Rope* (East Sussex, UK: The Ivy Press, 2003), 75.
3. Kennedy, *99 Tips*, 83.
4. Barbara Rolley, "Bodies in Motion," *Parenting*, September 2002, 86.

6: Twenty-Two to Twenty-Four Months

1. Scott Turansky and Joanne Miller, found at www.effectiveparenting.com, 2002.
2. Aletha Solter, "No More Tantrums," *Parenting*, February 2002, 88.

3. Turansky and Miller.

4. Allie Pleiter, *Becoming a Chief Home Officer: Thriving in Your "Career Shift" to Stay-at-Home Mom* (Grand Rapids, Mich.: Zondervan, 2002), 116.

7: Twenty-Four to Twenty-Six Months

1. Jay Cerio, Ph.D., quoted in Deborah Skolnik, "Let's Make Believe," *Parenting,* September 2003, 218.

2. Iovine, *Guide to Toddlers,* 113.

3. Trent et al., *Spiritual Growth,* 284.

8: Twenty-Six to Twenty-Eight Months

1. Tracy Hogg with Melinda Blau, *Secrets of the Baby Whisperer for Toddlers* (New York: Ballantine, 2002), 3.

2. Lauren Slater, "How Children Learn About Love," *Parenting,* February 2002, 74.

9: Twenty-Eight to Thirty Months

1. Harriet Griffey, *Your Toddler from 2 to 3: A Step-by-Step Guide for Parents* (New York: DK Publishing, 2002), 49.

2. Michael Mount, quoted in Lisa Lombardi, "Scream Savers," *Child,* March 2001, 76.

3. Hogg, *Baby Whisperer for Toddlers,* 53.

10: Thirty to Thirty-Two Months

1. Peter Downey, *Dads, Toddlers and the Chicken Dance* (Tucson: Fisher Books, 2000), 76.

2. Downey, *Chicken Dance,* 17.

11: Thirty-Two to Thirty-Four Months

1. Dave Barry, "Baby Love—or Why Childcare Is a Publishing Gold Mine," *Miami Herald,* November 10, 2001.

2. Nathan H. Azrin and Richard M. Foxx, *Toilet Training in Less Than a Day* (New York: Pocket Books, 1974), 50-1.

3. Azrin and Foxx, *Toilet Training,* 51.

4. Azrin and Foxx, *Toilet Training,* 54.

5. Azrin and Foxx, *Toilet Training,* 55.

6. Trent et al., *Spiritual Growth,* 278.

7. Pleiter, *Chief Home Officer,* 107.

8. Pleiter, *Chief Home Officer,* 119.

9. Pleiter, *Chief Home Officer,* 112.

12: Thirty-Four to Thirty-Six Months

1. Paula Spencer, "Mother Knows Best," *Family Circle Magazine,* April 24, 2001, 142.

2. Marianne Neifert, "Spirituality and Your Child," found at www.parentcenter.com, 2002.

3. *My Son's Blessing Book* (Colorado Springs: WaterBrook, 2001), 2.

4. Hogg, *Baby Whisperer for Toddlers,* 6.

LORILEE CRAKER is pictured here as a thirty-something bridesmaid, clutching two wild-and-woolly ring bearers before they tip over the unity candle or break a wedding present. The little guy is Ezra, whose foibles and fabulousness are chronicled in these pages, and the guy with the cheesy grin is Jonah, the big brother. In this photo, Ez is two and a half, and Jonah is five and a half. Both have recently turned one year older.

Doyle, Lorilee's longsuffering husband, is making a dash for the little church reception buffet table. The much-ballyhooed event was the wedding of Lorilee's friends Rachel and Jeff. (Cropped out are the bride and groom, looking at each other in a goopy way.)

Now that Rachel has moved to Missouri, Lorilee is in the market for new single friends to live vicariously through, attend chick flicks with, and to possibly even serve as a "mature" bridesmaid for. (Hey, it's a chance to get her hair done!) Captured for posterity, this picture was taken in Grand Rapids, Michigan, on a sunny summer day.